CHASED BY SPARROWS

Thank you for your support!

Caleb M

Chased By Sparrows

Caleb Madison
Katya Madison

By Wisdom Home

Contents

Nine

To my wonderful wife, whose art,
editing, and determination made this
book possible.

Preface

I spent my college years preoccupied by thoughts of telling the world of Jesus' love. Most days, I went to class distracted, rarely applying myself. During my junior year of college, I got a job as a resident assistant at my university, but I couldn't help but feel that my purpose was lying far beyond the borders of my campus, and I longed to fulfill it. Thoughts of philosophy and Christ never left my mind, as they were my only window to gaze out at a purpose beyond what my everyday life offered. I tried to write a book several times over the years, but each time I found that I did not know enough, and I always wondered why someone—beyond my family and friends—would care about what I had to say.

These thoughts kept me from pursuing writing for some time until one day, I was sitting at the entrance to the residence hall with my fellow resident assistants when they asked to hear a story. I can't quite remember why they had asked or why I chose to tell this particular story, but I told them of how I fell in love with my now wife. Our love story was full of odd twists and turns that were comical in a shocking kind of way. Let's just say, I was not the most perceptive individual in the world. How they all listened with intense interest caught my attention. Previously, I had tried to share God's love with each of them separately. They had all told me 'no,' in a variety of ways and so, it had become clear to me they were not interested in hearing about Jesus.

Not this time. This time, they wanted to hear what I had to say, and they were hanging on every word. I decided I needed to weave Christ's love into the story as I went. This particular task was not difficult, as Christ's love was already at the heart of the story. When I had spoken to them about Jesus in the past, I spoke using apologetic and philosophical arguments rather than preaching the heart of the Gospel. They did not care much for my arguments; their minds were already made up. God was not real to them, and it did not matter if there were mountains of archaeological evidence in support of the Bible. They did not feel the gravity of Jesus' love, but when I spoke of my love for Katya, they all longed to hear what I had to say. I believe the love I spoke of awakened something in them and I believe that thing exists within each of us. They, like me, desired to be loved. They wanted to be fulfilled and they were currently lacking that fulfillment. They seemed to have a deep and abiding belief that their fulfillment would be found in the arms of another person, but I knew the love they were seeking would only be found when they came into right relationship with their Creator. This desire for love and to be loved is a divine addition to the human psyche. Old Nat King Cole wrote a song called Nature Boy and in it he says, "the greatest thing you'll ever learn is just to love and be loved in return." I believe this is true, but what is greater than love alone is love shared with the source of all love, Jesus.

For years, I had been trying to tell the story of Jesus' love through a medium that I did not fully understand. I wanted to write a book that showed Jesus was God but every time I approached this topic with a nonfiction mindset, I quickly became discouraged. As I looked at what I had written, I realized that hundreds of Christians had already penned what I was writing, and they had done a much better job, too. As I told the story of how I fell in love with my girlfriend though, I realized something. They wanted to hear a story. My whole life, I have always understood reality as a story. As I traveled to and from school, I imagined worlds outside my own. I turned over a single narrative in my mind for months, refining the story and exploring the world through thought. Each story reflected some desire I was wrestling with, and each story helped me to reach a conclusion about life. I understood everything in terms of story, and I was beginning to realize that many other people did as well.

There are few people who want to sit down and read a dense book of peer reviewed studies critiquing antibiotics and their merits, but millions of people loved watching the hit show *House*. Story changes everything. A story may not have actually happened, but the ideas communicated can sometimes reveal truths that no list of facts could ever attempt to express. I realized that just because something is called fiction, does not mean it's not true. Stories have the ability to communicate a deeper reality and they can do so in an enjoyable manner. Perhaps this is why God chose to reveal Himself primarily in terms of a story, and not just a list of facts.

This book sets out to do just that. I mean to write a book that follows two parallel love stories. The story of a man and a woman finding true love, and the story of a man finding his love for God again. This book is meant to show one thing: God's love. I am not a theologian, and I do not have degree in philosophy, nor in English. I am only a man who loves stories and loves God. This is not meant to be a critique of theology or a book on apologetics. If that is what you want, you will not find it here. This is a love story through and through.

One

Winter's Cab

Nathan shivered as he stood on the sidewalk beside an old abandoned house. The bitter cold pierced his cheeks and he thrust his hands deep into his pockets. The cab pulled next to the curb; Nathan ducked his head and slid into the back seat. His movements were muted from prolonged exposure to the cold. His teeth chattered violently causing his jaw to ache. The temperature was so unbearable that Nathan had not stopped to speak to the driver before getting in the car. Now, he leaned forward, handing the driver an address. The driver took it and started away from the curb. Nathan, now warming in the vehicle, loosened the hood of his coat and brushed it off his head. He gazed out the window of the old Ford as it barreled down the highway through the countryside. The driver looked back as if to say something but returned his gaze to the road. Nathan turned away from the front of the car, crossed his arms and slouched in his seat.

The house lingered in Nathan's mind. He remembered a time when its sight would fill his heart with joy. He longed for the days when only a thought of it could warm even the coldest night. Now, it filled Nathan's mind with sadness. Jobs gained and lost, bills paid and left unpaid, health and sickness, fights and making up were all held in those four walls. His old house still stood with no one left inside: the joy was missing, the love gone, the life ended. The image grew sharp and distinct in his mind as he began to recall every detail of his visit. Its broken windows, old shutters, and cracked paint showed its age. Ivy grew over the door and around the light fixtures on either side of a stained-glass window in the center door. The stained-glass had almost brought tears to his eyes. The hawk depicted was so elegant, strong, and fearless. Nathan had not felt like that hawk in years. He then thought of the living room. There was a shadow over the fireplace where a picture once hung. A discoloration on the wall created a square of empty space that longed to be filled. The dust and cobwebs that hung in each corner obscured the beauty of the room.

Nathan remembered walking down a hallway that started from the living room and stretched to the kitchen. When had he entered the kitchen, he longed to smell the sweet aromas that used to emanate from this room. At that moment, all he could smell was dust and the faint odor of a mouse droppings. The old hand-carved cabinets loosely hung from the wall and threatened to fall off at even the slightest disturbance. Nathan turned to see notches carved in the door frame that rose to about four feet high. The notches grew further apart as they rose and the full names displayed at the bottom turned to only initials at the top.

Nathan did not linger here for long and instead walked to the base of the staircase. He took one uneasy step onto the first stair; the whole house creaked. He remembered the fear that filled his heart at this moment. He was not sure if the staircase would hold him, but he took another step. This time his front foot went through the wood and he fell forward. He reached out his hands to protect his face and managed to stop his fall. He slowly stood up and pulled his foot from the hole. Nathan's desire to see the house vanished and he made his way to the front door. He stood in the doorway for what felt like an eternity, just staring out of the house as if he was waiting for someone to return home, but no one came.

A single tear fell from Nathan's eye. He was glad to have left that place, but he felt he had left behind far more than just a house. It was not clear to Nathan just what he left there, but he felt empty. He had abandoned something great and he wondered if he would ever recover it again.

Unprovoked, the driver began to speak. "Have you ever had the realization that God is not simply an argument to win, a pretty story to tell, or a useful tool for philosophers?" The driver paused, and Nathan, confused, sat up to listen. The driver had only just begun to speak and yet it seemed as if he were return-ing to a familiar debate. "Have you ever been struck, all at once, with the idea that God is real? I mean, that He is *really* there?" The driver asked the questions with such joy Nathan could see tears welling up in his eyes. "God is real. I don't need to defend him to anyone... to myself, even." Nathan did not respond but instead, he detected a hint of surprise in the face of the driver as if he hadn't intended to say what he had. The driver's hands began to shake on the wheel, and Nathan could almost feel the man's heart pounding. It was clear that he had not responded the way the driver had hoped.

Nathan was taken aback by the passion that had brought this man to the verge of tears, and he wondered why this passion was being directed toward him. *Does this man think there is something wrong with me?* he asked himself.

"I had to ask myself, what has caused the peace I now have," the driver continued, "and how had I reached a point where skepticism would no longer strangle my faith? I was looking for scientific proof God exists, as most people these days are. Or perhaps, they merely demand proof without a willingness to search for it. This venture, though, is nothing more than a fool's errand. God cannot be measured, tested, or repeated. What nonsense I used to demand of God. God is not any more a piece of His creation than a builder a wall in his house."

"I had not yet realized certainty itself is a fool's errand. At least, when it comes to the natural world. In science, we say 'the evidence suggests that'…we never say 'prove.' Scientists look at the aggregate of data they have collected and draw an inference, knowing full well they have an infinitesimal portion of all the data that could have been collected. 'Prove' is a word for blogs and opinion journalists, not for true science. So, in this way, I could never be certain. I could never prove there is or is not a God. 'What's the point?' I asked myself, 'shouldn't we all just be agnostics?'" The old man paused and breathed deeply. He had lost his breath from talking so quickly and his breathing had become heavy and labored. There was a slight rasp behind every word, but the driver was not deterred; instead, he slowed his speech and continued, "You may say to yourself, 'I would never be so dogmatic as to say there is no God, but I wouldn't change my entire life to serve a god I cannot know.' In a vacuum, this point of view may seem reasonable, but we are not in a vacuum. Science may be thoroughly unequipped to answer the question of why, but that doesn't mean this question is unanswerable. We have available to us our reasonable faculties, philosophy, and perhaps most powerfully, our own inner experience."

"Now, you may feel keen to dismiss Christians as people who believe based on blind faith, as I once did. You may also determine you are far too intelligent to ever believe something so ridiculous and ill-founded as the resurrection of Christ but indulge me. What if, while proof is unattainable, there was evidence? What if while you cannot see God, you can experience Him? What if while you may not be able to speak directly with God, He made himself evident in this world? What if Christians are not merely closing their eyes and leaping, but are seeing clearly and trusting? I asked myself these questions, and it led me down a path I would have never expected." The driver looked down at his lap. "I cannot answer every question that has ever been asked of God. I am not able to dispel every last rogue thought raised against the cross. But I can tell you the story of a man whose skepticism was at last put to death by the power of Christ. I want you to hear how God changed the heart of one man. In my story, the hero loves the villain, and the villain's greatest crime is not loving the hero back."

Nathan scanned the car for anything to pay attention to other than the wild-eyed man; he did not want to encourage the driver to continue his ramblings. The driver stared intently into the rearview mirror as if penetrating Nathan's hard exterior and seeing the man within. The driver was old, with long, deep, wrinkles across his cheeks. Bright blue eyes peered out from behind bushy eyebrows and a warm face covered in hair. He had dirt smudged across his forehead and he wore ratty and tattered clothing. The car shook and rattled with the slightest unevenness of the road. Nathan briefly feared for his life when the driver, looking back in the rearview mirror, struck a pothole straight on. The car shook so violently Nathan nearly expected it to fall to pieces in the middle of the road. He wished he had just stayed home.

Nathan retreated into his mind. *This man is just another person touched in the head by the poison of religion. He clearly gave up whatever ability he had to think critically in exchange for joyful ignorance. Then again, perhaps this man is just lonely and desperate for someone to talk to. Maybe I'll listen. After all, I have nothing else to do but to sit and hear him rant.* Nathan stopped searching for a distraction from the driver and turned his full attention upon him.

"You're back," the driver said with a grin.

"Agh, what do you mean?" Nathan asked sharply.

The driver did not answer, shook his head, and looked away from the mirror. He wore a crooked smile and his right eyelid sagged. Though he looked unkempt and disheveled, the joy emanating from behind his eyes was unmistakable; it was the kind of joy that comes when a long-awaited goal is met, or when a prize has been won. This joy began to anger Nathan. *How dare this old man assume I need something from him. Here he is, driving a car for a living. What unbridled arrogance he has.*

Nathan prepared to tell the driver exactly how he felt when he heard the old man say,

"Sorry for the rattle in my car. I took it into the shop just the other day, and I was told the car is on its way out...." The driver paused as if to cry. Nathan looked at him, surprised by the emotion in his voice. He choked back his tears and spoke with renewed clarity, "Anyway, it wouldn't be worth fixing, so I just let it be. Would you believe I've had this car since freshman year of college?"

The driver's question was disarming to Nathan. *College?* Nathan thought, surprised. *If this man went to college, why was he driving a car for a living?* Nathan's anger at the man slowly dissipated and was replaced with a newfound curiosity. Nathan turned his gaze to the barren cornfields passing by outside his window.

"Beautiful, isn't it?"

"Yes, beautiful," Nathan answered sarcastically and then added, "It certainly doesn't smell beautiful, though."

The driver gave a shallow chuckle and continued to stare out of the driver's side window. *How was he doing that?* Nathan marveled to himself. The driver had the uncanny ability to barely look at the road in front of him. It seemed that he was always looking at the fields or in the rearview mirror, but never the road.

Both men sat in silence until Nathan heard himself ask aloud, "Where did you go to college?"

At once, the old man began to seem more youthful to Nathan. He pulled his gaze from the cornfields and placed it on the rearview mirror. "Oxford."

"How did you end up here, like this?" Nathan asked, and immediately felt he had been too harsh. He meant to apologize and retract the question when the driver smiled and said, "That's a long story, my friend."

Nathan heard himself say, "Well, this is gonna be a long ride, and I'm interested." As the words left his mouth, he wondered why he said them. The driver had offered him a way out, a chance to sit in silence, but he continued the conversation and gave the him license to talk. Was it out of guilt, pity, true fascination, or something else? Having sealed his fate for the remainder of the drive, Nathan settled back into his seat and peered out the window on his right. The driver leaned forward and turned on the radio and began to hum along.

"Do you ever think? I mean *really* think?" The driver asked suddenly. "Have you ever questioned everything, or found yourself thinking nothing is real at all? Like the world is only a lie? I wondered about this and it was not a light burden to bear. What brings a man to this point? What makes him question everything this way? Perhaps these pains are invoked by some tragedy, like the death of a loved one, or a betrayal of some kind? For me, it was nothing quite so monumental; I first questioned everything because of sex."

"Sex?!" Nathan's head snapped around to face the driver and his posture became upright.

"Yes, sex." The driver answered matter-of-factly. "I wanted to have it."

Nathan, now exceedingly uncomfortable with the direction of the conversation, could not help but be paradoxically, yet increasingly fascinated by every word that came from the driver.

"The only problem was," the driver continued, unfazed by Nathan's outburst, "I was a Christian. There was no major life event that caused me to question reality; there was only tension between two great desires. I had to know if I was doing the right thing by restraining myself. It was not a very noble search, I admit, but it was the beginning of my search for truth and I believe I have found it. I don't remember every word I heard, every event that took place, and every person that taught me something along the way, but I sense you are not keen to hear all of that anyway. You are tired, I can tell. You don't want studies and peer-reviewed journals. You want to hear a story." Nathan said nothing, but he knew the driver was right. He wanted to hear a story.

Two

Misplaced

"Do you remember when I was young?" asked the driver.

What does he mean, 'do I remember?' Nathan thought, but the question quickly vanished from his mind as the man spoke in a fast cadence.

"Everything seemed simple. Everything seemed right or wrong. Do you remember believing easily? Do you remember what it meant to trust? I often wish I could return to my youth. I wish for the sun to shine again. It has not shone in here for years. I wish to again feel the sun's warmth on my skin. I want to be home again. I had full trust I was safe, true, and loved when I was inside. Somewhere along the line, I lost that place. I lost that trust, that faith. Do you remember losing your home?" The driver paused and began to hum again.

Nathan wanted to tell the driver exactly when he lost his faith and his home, and he opened his mouth to tell the driver, but before he could speak, he realized he could not remember. Nathan wracked his mind. He knew he had lost his faith, and he knew he had a multitude of good reasons for it too, but at that moment, he could not remember a single one.

The driver continued, "I used to wonder at the world before I decided I knew everything. Of course, back then I never claimed to know everything aloud. If someone were to ask me, I would feign humility and speak of the expanse of the universe and the unknowable nature of truth, but secretly, I always believed I knew everything worth knowing. As a child, this lie had not yet gripped my heart. I was free to inquire and wonder at the world without the necessity to posture I already knew the answer I sought." The driver's speech trailed off and it became difficult to make out. Nathan leaned forward to hear the man better, but the driver had returned to humming.

Nathan sank back into his seat, and decided to join the driver in his song. *What was this song?* Nathan asked himself. *Was this the same song that was playing when the driver turned the radio on? It was familiar. Yes, yes it was. More than that, was this is the only song that'd been played up to this point?* But Nathan, despite straining to hear, could not quite make out the words.

"Love," the man proclaimed.

"Love?"

"Love. It is why I believe. You may say I am basing my entire life on a meaningless construct. It's nothing more than pleasure hormones and neurotransmitters, after all, but I think once you have loved and been loved, I mean *truly*loved, you will find that love is more real than your very thoughts."

So, he was a romantic. He will spout meaningless niceties. They may even appear to be intellectual, but I know better, Nathan thought.

But Nathan, almost against his will, spoke, "I have loved, and it is nothing like what you say. I have cared for...someone...to their death. I watched over them and sat by their side for days, weeks even. I have shown love and I tell you, love did not drive me to faith."

"But why?"

"Because I loved her, don't you see?" Nathan said with malice behind his words. He was surprised with himself. Why was he sharing so much, and why was he so angry? This man had done nothing, but Nathan could not control his rage, and he repeated himself with even more anger. "I loved her. I wanted her to be at peace more than I wanted my own peace. I would have given anything for her to be at peace!"

"Isn't that real? Don't you feel that deep within your soul? Don't you know with every fiber of your being that your love for her was more, *is* more?"

Nathan paused for a moment. Perhaps this man was right. His love did seem to feel more real than all other experiences. Nathan felt his face begin to soften. The thought of the love he shared awakened a feeling deep within, but as he thought of her, flashes of her death began to fill his mind. His momentary feelings of love vanished in the face of the pain that still strangled his heart. *Love does not explain my pain.* Nathan suppressed his anger and he spoke to the driver in a low, calm voice.

"No, it was a lie, just like all the rest. Your 'God' took her from me, after all. So, the mere fact that you Christians believe He is love... means I must hate Him and your broken idea of 'love.'"

Nathan let out a groan and turned away to face the back of the vehicle. He wished this man would stop the car to let him out, but he could not bring himself to say the words. In his anger, Nathan found himself torn. Part of him wanted to leave, to get out of the car and be done with the man, but another part, the part beneath the hurt, wanted the driver to continue.

"I met her freshman year of college. Do you remember? She sat next to me every day." the driver stated. "She was pretty, but my arrogance told me she was for some lesser man. She spoke incisively, with cutting perceptions of the world around her. This made what she said funny, but when she spoke you did not want to laugh exactly. Maybe it was much more like you became captivated by her presence and you were left with nothing but intrigue. She was the kind of girl that left a thought in your mind well after she had gone." *Who is that girl?*

Nathan thought he was beginning to remember who the driver was describing, and embarrassment rose within him. *Am I confused?* Nathan worried.

"I spoke to her every day, and I believe I probably drove her to the brink of insanity." The driver beamed and looked back in the mirror with a twinkle in his eye. "She certainly did not like me, but she talked to me, so I kept talking. I quickly found that she was a Buddhist, and my interest in her waned. She could make a good friend, I decided. It wasn't long before she was dating my best friend whose resolve against dating non-Christians was not quite as strong as mine." The man rolled his eyes and chuckled again. Nathan observed something quite peculiar about this laugh. He recalled the driver's laugh as shallow; almost like a kind of courtesy laugh you might award someone who attempted a cheap pun while noticeably proud of their own wit. This laugh was different. He laughed with his whole body. It began in his cheeks and then his shoulders. One shoulder, quickly followed by the other, raised and lowered. This was an odd motion and it struck Nathan as familiar, but he could not quite place its source.

"Why—" Nathan cleared his throat, his voice was shaky with concern he was losing his mind. "Why should being a Buddhist matter?"

"Faith."

"Faith?"

"Indeed."

"I'm sorry, sir, but I'm afraid you must be much clearer than that," Nathan exclaimed, frustrated by the unnecessary back and forth.

"Well, I was not yet sure God was real, but I was trying to live as if I was. I wanted to protect my faith."

"Don't you think if your faith could so easily be lost, it was not worth having?'

"Many things easily lost are worth having," the driver paused, "Maybe some of the most important things are easily lost. Whatever the case, the way we Christians see the world is odd. There's nothing quite like it. So, I concluded that if she did not see the world the way I was trying to, we would not match."

This answer satisfied Nathan. It was the first thing the driver said that made any sense to him. It was as if the driver was becoming more real as he spoke. He seemed cleaner, clearer, and perhaps... younger. Yes, his eyes appeared to be more youthful than Nathan had previously thought.

"Well, soon enough I told her how I felt about her dating my friend. It was truly an odd situation. One day, out of the blue, she asked if I approved and as you probably already know, I said no. I was shocked to see pain in her eyes. She wanted my approval. I could see it. But I did not know why; after all, she clearly did not like me very much. Why would she? All I did was annoy her. It had become one of my favorite pastimes, and it was clearly not one of her's. I could not tell why she cared about my opinion, but when I told her, she cried! I was stupefied. *This girl, who would rather I did not exist as part of her life, was crying because I did not approve of her relationship,* I thought, but I was not seeing the whole picture. Her tears had little to do with me; her heart ached because she feared taking my friend's faith. How could you blame her? That's what I told her, after all. I would not and did not approve of her dating my friend because she was going to ruin him. Now, I am not quite sure if this truly reflected how I felt, but it is what she heard, and so her emotion, instead of driving her to end the relationship with my friend, drove her to consider Christianity. Can you believe that? I somehow stumbled right into sharing the story of Jesus' love. This was unbelievably odd because I, myself, did not yet believe in such a story, at least not fully."

"Well, she went off and asked questions, read books, and watched preachers, and before long, came back to me and said, 'Well, what if I am a Buddhist who likes Christian things?' I did not budge. I said, 'No good.' She left and did more thinking. Then, she came back to me and proclaimed triumphantly she was now a 'Christian-Buddhist.' I laughed at her, and said, 'You might as well call yourself a 19-year-old octogenarian. You can't be two conflicting things at once.'

The driver paused. "I can see you are confused, what is it?"

"You say you did not believe Christianity yourself, yet you behaved as if you were certain of it."

"Yes, well, I didn't need to believe in the resurrection and all other manner of Christian doctrine to see a contradiction in terms, now did I?

"But what did you believe? Didn't you also hold contradictions?"

"Yes, I did, and they were eating away to me. Although, this did not stop me from critiquing others. I could tell someone to clean up after themselves in the most indignant manner and then to also leave a mess the very same instance. It was of no consequence to me."

Nathan did not speak again but instead motioned with his hand for the driver to continue.

"Well anyway, she left again, frustrated by my input, and this time she stopped checking in with me altogether. It was weeks later when she called herself a Christian in passing and I, shocked by this new revelation, grabbed her arm and demanded more clarity. She looked me in the eye and explained that she was now a Christian. Apparently, she had hesitated to tell me because she didn't want me to feel I had won the argument. After all, she had decided on her own. I did not win her and that was true enough. So, I let it be—for the most part. Of course, there were times in our lives when I reminded her that I had been right about the most important thing in the world while she was wrong. But, for the sake of our relationship, I mostly avoided those moments. It was not long after this declaration when she broke up with my best friend. It seemed her new-found Christianity had driven a wedge between them. Perhaps he was not quite as Christian as she."

The car rolled to a stop, and the driver took a deep breath. He turned to Nathan and said, "I won't be a minute." He got out of the car and began to relieve himself on the field next to the highway. As Nathan waited, he could not help but feel he had forgotten something very important. He assured himself he was fine, and he had everything he needed, but the uneasy feeling would not leave. The driver stepped back into the car, turned up the heat, and waited for a chance to jump back into traffic. Without pausing, he plunged back into his narrative.

"It was about that time when I also decided God was real, or at least I couldn't prove He wasn't. I simply lived as if He existed because I felt the stakes would be far too high if I was wrong. You know, burning in Hell and such. Anyway, I began to get my life in order. I read the Bible almost every day and I stopped doing some things—well, you know. I felt I had my life on the right track and it was about time God did something for me. As I mentioned earlier, I wanted to have sex, and because I decided I was a Christian, I was waiting for marriage. There was only one problem I could not find myself a suitable woman. Now, you may say, what about the girl? She was a Christian now, right? All that is true, but I can honestly say ever since the first time I saw her, a thought of her in that way had never crossed my mind, at least unprovoked. Instead, I dated every beautiful woman I could find. I must have dated sixty women."

"Sixty?!" Nathan asked, hardly believing the driver.

"Fine, maybe not quite sixty, but the likes of it. This world was crawling with beautiful women, but for some reason, none of them struck my fancy past their exterior. This, of course, did not matter fully; I was still willing to try and make it work. At a certain point, I got fed up with things not going the way I intended, and I concluded that I would never meet a girl I wanted to marry unless God did something about it. So, I told the big man I had done quite a lot for Him, and it was time He returned the favor. Would you guess that all He gave me were unrelenting thoughts of being with that girl? Not in any kind of sexual way, mind you, but just being with her. Every time I closed my eyes, there she was—fully clothed, I might add. When I went to sleep, I dreamt of her. It was positively nauseating how often that girl showed her face in my thoughts. I began to feel as if my mind had been hijacked by God. I begged Him to stop, but it only got worse. Well, worse in the sense that I thought of her more often. So, I resolved to fight back. God could not have my thoughts, and so I took to searching for another girl to occupy them. I found many, each of them wonderful, or at least I convinced myself they were. Each time I found a new girl, it started wonderfully, but within a few weeks, they would suddenly realize they never truly liked me and would leave.

"If you were having thoughts of the girl, why not just date her?"

"Because they were not mine."

"But they were in your head, weren't they?"

"Yes, but they were not mine. I did not want to give my will over to God. My will would win, and His would not. This was *my* life, and I would do as *I* pleased."

"But didn't you say you were living for Him?"

"Sure, I gave the parts of myself that were easy to give. I refrained from lying, cheating, and beating people when it suited me, but I never gave my full will."

"But why not?"

"Because I was not truly a Christian. I had not yet confessed He was Lord, that I was Servant and He was Master. I think you probably know I no longer feel that way, but at the time, I did. My will rebelled against the idea of letting another decide my fate. I and I alone was god. Of course, I see this idea as nothing more than youthful folly now, but it was all so real to me back then. After a while, all this turmoil came to its culmination when I left for a summer. I decided to go hiking, so I got a backpack, food, and a tent, and I left. I spent three long months wandering the mountains alone."

"It's a bit dramatic, don't you think? You couldn't find a girl you liked, is all. It's not like the world was ending, or anything."

"Alright then, have you ever overreacted before?" the driver asked playfully, feigning annoyance.

Nathan paused, "I—I don't know." He stammered. Nathan was not being difficult. He really could not seem to remember anything of his past, let alone a time he overreacted. *What's wrong with me?* Nathan thought. He looked at his hands and turned them over. *I'm certainly here, why can't I remember?* But the driver, unaware of Nathan's confusion, continued talking. Nathan, trying to focus on his lack of memory, could feel himself being pulled back into the driver's story. He could not divert his attention for even one second; it was as if all of his senses were screaming to hear every feeble word that fell from the driver's tongue, so Nathan did not resist.

"I yelled, hit trees, and even contemplated ending my life. What did my life mean if I had no control over it? Every decision I made had to be mine. It had to be. I yelled at God. I demanded to know why He thought He could tell me what to do. 'What gives you the right?' I snarled. For months I got on that way with no response. Not even the slightest message."

"Then one day, I was sitting on a cliff telling God one last time how I had served Him well and I asked, 'God why won't you send me my wife?' In a flash, I was a child. I don't mean I merely *remembered* being a child. I *was* a child, and I heard my mother moving furniture downstairs. I leapt out of bed and began to run towards the staircase, but I paused. It was a school day and I did not yet have my uniform on. I quickly got dressed and crept down the stairs so as not to wake my brother. I did not want him to wake and join me because I wanted the credit for being a good son, alone. I found my spot at the table, pulled out my chair, and sat with my hands folded in front of me. My mother, hearing the chair move, came to the kitchen. As soon as I saw her, I said, 'I'll have waffles.'

"I was so proud. I had awoken, gotten dressed, and chosen my breakfast all on my own. I was expecting my mother to be pleased as well because I was typically a terror in the morning. I hid under my covers when it was time to wake, I resisted putting on a uniform, objecting that it was scratchy, and when my mother or father had finally won and had gotten me to the kitchen, I could never decide what I wanted to eat. Not this morning. This morning, I was a good son. My mother looked at me with such love that I felt I had truly done right. In that moment I even pondered a future of always being an obedient son. I was full. The feeling was brought to an early conclusion when I heard my mother's laughter and then her voice telling me, through her tears, to go back to bed, it is only ten o'clock. When I awoke from my vision realized that I had been inside a memory and I remembered why my mother had laughed. I had gone to bed at seven and awoken only three hours later when I heard my mother preparing to go to bed herself."

"I was returned to my body with two new thoughts that seemed implanted in my mind. The first was, 'you will have your waffles, but not quite yet.' The second was so clear and real that I have never felt or known anything else quite like it: 'I love you.' He had answered me and I was satisfied. I realize now He could have said anything. It did not matter to me, I just needed to hear Him. I stood, packed my things, and left the cliff never to return to its edge again."

"Upon my arrival home, I was met with numerous letters from the girl. Many of these letters were benign and said nothing of consequence. As I looked through them, they seemed to be a record of all the things she thought and felt while I was away. I must have had a hundred of these letters. It appears as if there was one for each day I was gone, and even two on days where she had an extraordinary amount to say to me. I sat down in my living room, placed them in order of date, and began to read." The driver stopped talking and began to cough violently.

He reached into his glove compartment and rustled his hand around for a few moments before he pulled out a handful of envelopes. He reached back to Nathan, and Nathan took the envelopes. Nathan held six envelopes, each of them decorated with a different scene. His eyes checked the date on each, set aside the five most recent, pulled the paper from the sixth and began to read.

Three

Willow Trees

The letters flew from the page like a frightened flock of birds. Nathan's heart raced and his breathing became irregular. He wiped his eyes, hoping to clear the illusion, but when he removed his hands, the words only spun faster. The sound of wind was whirling about him and Nathan clenched his eyes shut, hoping when they were opened, the world would make sense again. Suddenly, Nathan was only aware of the paper in his hands. He opened his eyes and the words of the letter now drifted slowly back and forth. The driver was a thought laying just beyond his grasp, his existence was a lifetime ago. Nathan looked at the first line of the letter, attempting to force his eyes to focus on to whom the letter was addressed. He saw, "Dear..." but the remainder of the line eluded his full comprehension. Frustrated, he turned to see what was drawn on the exterior of the envelope. The scene was illustrated with a single black ink pen. Depicted were two willow trees standing over a bench. The bench overlooked a pond filled with fish, turtles, and dragonflies. Children raced up and down its banks discovering each creature that called the pond its home. Nathan felt warmth fill his heart, but it was unclear why. He supposed this image had caused it. His frustration at being unable to interpret the name on the letter dissolved when he became aware of the first line.

Dear ------,

I am unsure why I decided to write to you. I do not mean any offense by this, of course, but, as you know, I am not one for making waves in otherwise still waters. Furthermore, I have never done anything quite like this before. I mean, of course, I have written letters in the past, but not for this purpose.

I have many reasons to doubt whether this letter will find you. Primarily, I do not know where you are, and even if I did, I imagine you will not be checking your mail. Even so, I figure writing my thoughts down could not hurt. I suppose, after all, I am not certain I will even send this, but if I do...well, I am sure you will find my motives genuine.

I am already thankful for these letters because I feel my meaning is often lost in speech. My points are obfuscated by my lack of immediate clarity, and once more by the louder and more boisterous people in the room. I do not mean to sound like a poor helpless girl, because, as you well know, I am not one of those, but sometimes I fear my insecurities, however well I hide them, prevent me from standing my ground amongst wrong ideas, especially when they are asserted loudly and with passion. So, I quite like this method of communication. Of course, this way, you cannot interrupt me to tell me I am wrong before

I have made my entire point. I jest, but I am sure you knew that. The thought just occurred to me—perhaps this is why so few people these days read. I mean, I think many people must believe the louder they speak, the more correct they are, and I also suspect they have very little interest in hearing another's perspective all the way through anyway.

In any event, I didn't know what I wanted my first letter to contain, and as you can see, I've just started rambling. After a few failed attempts to compose a letter to you, I told myself whatever came to my head I would write. I sure hope I do not bore you, but if I do, oh well; worse things have happened. Once I began placing my words on this page, I realized it would be far better if I had a direction. (this I wrote after sitting a while) I have found a direction, but I think I will still allow myself to wander along the way, and I am sure you will allow me that privilege as well. Please, do not think I am aimless because I am not. Here, on this page, I intend to ask questions of my aim, which as you know, is now and will always be God. I pray that God, or you, either, I suppose, will not take my thoughts as blaspheme; I only wish to put to paper the questions I have been asking inside my mind.

Do you remember the day when you took me to the pond by the willows? We sat on the bench on the peninsula in the middle of the pond. We ate food and watched the little children fish for minnows. You told me something back then that, at the time, made me cringe. You said my life is not my own, and so, almost instinctively, we began to argue (that is what we did in those days). "How can my life be anyone else's? It's in the phrase "my life" that I am the owner. There is no joint contract for ownership, no wretched slave owner, and certainly not any man I would allow to direct my life. So, why are you sitting here telling me my life was not my own?" I believe I said something of the sort. Of course, now I can't fully remember what we said, but I cannot help but wonder if we got it quite wrong back then. Is it true my life is not my own? If it is, then are my choices also someone else's? If so, how can God hold me accountable for my, for lack of a better word, choices? Of course, you see the flaw here, don't you? If my choices are programmed into me, you could not hold me accountable for my mistakes any more than you hold a lion accountable for killing a zebra. It was in my nature. Now, I know what you will say, you would laugh in the way you do and say, "Just because a thing is natural to a man, doesn't mean it's good for him." And, of course, you are right. For instance, it may naturally occur that a man is born with webbed feet which is not good, but I am not arguing against this. I am questioning whether or not that webbed-footed man can be held accountable for his webbed toes if possession of them were sinful, since, after all, he did nothing cause himself to be born with them. Now, I have also heard people say it is not true that my life not being my own means, necessarily, I cannot choose. To them, I say, "Well, then what does it mean?" I am quite sure whatever answer they may provide to this question must negate one of two points. Either I can choose, and my choices are my own, or I cannot choose, and God is unjust to hold me to account.

Now, I have taken a great deal of time to determine how it is possible for my life to not be my own, and also, for there to be a just God holding me accountable for my mistakes. This is what I found. First, I and all mankind have free will, and our lives are, indeed, ours, but they are not deserved. This I feel is necessary to maintain God's goodness, though many good people have held differing opinion. Secondly, our lives are a gift, and just like every other good thing in this world, they are from God. Now, it is true I have free will, and yet I can use my free will to give my life back to God so that now, it is not my own. So, when a Christian says "my life is not my own" they may be speaking truly, because they have given their life back to God. Furthermore, if a non-believer were to say that their life is their own, they are correct, but their sentiment often lacks the proper gratefulness for the gift they have received. This may be simple to you, but I feel it requires a great deal more explanation. So, allow me to start at the beginning.

God created everything, right? Okay, if this were so, then He also created man. The syllogism is as follows: God created everything, man is a thing, therefore, God created man. My logic is not flawed yet, and I hope you will afford me this relatively simple premise. Now, if He did indeed create man, then He must have had a reason to do so. Otherwise, we would be left with an irrational God, and I think the self-evident reason in the universe dispels that notion entirely. Now, to continue along this path of thought, we must first establish that God can be described. Of course, we say He is "indescribable" in many of our modern worship songs, but thank God this is not so, because otherwise, how could we know Him? Well, the idea of God being indescribable is patently false anyway, because the Bible is full of descriptions about God. Though, I will grant He can never be fully described because an infinite being cannot be contained by anything, much less by our feeble words. One description contained in the Bible says that He is loving.

This is important because to say God is loving is to also say God is not not loving. This is a definite description of what He is and what He is not. So, God is something, and He is also not something else. It would stand to reason, then, I could choose to love or not to love, which may be similar to saying I could choose God or not God. The thought then occurred to me, that perhaps this is what evil is. If God is good, and I do not mean merely His behavior is good, or good is only an accurate description of God, but that He is good, then evil would be defined as without God, because evil is the lack of good. The syllogism is as follows: God is good, good is fully without evil, God is without evil. The final premise could also be flipped as to say evil is without God. This idea put me at ease, at least partially. Before I had thought of this, I worried that perhaps God was evil, because how could something exist that God did not create? If God was evil, it would certainly explain why He would create beings, force them to sin, and then punish them for doing so. Furthermore, if God created evil, then He must Himself be evil because only an evil being would create evil, but here was my answer. Evil does not exist at all, or at the very least, it exists in a very different way than good does. Good is like my shirt, and evil is like the holes in my shirt. The holes only exist in the absence of my shirt material. So, when I choose evil, I am choosing nothing at all. I have chosen to exchange the truth of God for a lie. The real lie. Do you remember when we talked about the world being a lie? Well, I think I found the true lie, and it is not the world at all.

So, if it is true that God created man, that God is knowable, and that God is not evil then what does that mean for my life and free will?

Well, I think the gift of life is very much like if a father were to give an unassembled bicycle to his child. Sure, that bicycle now belongs to the child, but the child did not buy it, and the father still has ultimate authority over when, where, and how the bicycle is used. The father will allow the child to do whatever he wills with the bicycle parts, but what use do they serve unassembled? The child might decide to use the seat as a gun and then proceed to chase shadows yelling "freeze!" The child may also decide the chain is a pretty necklace and play dress-up with it. All the pieces of the bicycle may be used for any purpose the child likes, but a child does not know that each piece, when used properly, will have a purpose much greater than any single purpose he may create in the meantime. You may object and say the child is ignorant. How can the child know the pieces form a bicycle on his own? Of course, some children, the brightest, may determine there was some greater purpose to all those pieces, but even then, that child would never assume the purpose was to form a bicycle. That is why the father left an instruction manual. What is interesting about a child with an instruction manual is that even with that manual, the child will remain incapable of assembling the bicycle; he lacks the intellect and proper tools. That is why the front of the manual says 'adult assembly required.' After reading this manual, the child may ask the father to build the bicycle for him. In this case, the father will assemble the bicycle.

Once it is assembled though, the job is not finished. Many children will jump on the bike and ride it for a foot or two before crashing to the ground. These individuals may never return to the bicycle again; after all, how could a loving father let his child crash? Another child may pretend the bicycle is a horse. He may walk next to it for miles, too scared to get on, and as a result, that child will never experience the joy of riding the bicycle. Some children, though, will ask the father to show them how to ride the bicycle. In this way, they give up their freedom to play with it as they see fit. They exchange their perception of the use of the bike for the father's perception. These children will learn to ride, and they will also find that using the bike as a gun, necklace, or horse was far less satisfying than using it for the purpose for which it was designed. In this way, the bike is not the child's because the father has authority over the bike. It is true though, that he will not make us ride it. He won't even make us assemble it if we do not want to, and in this way, our bikes are our own. Being a Christian is about recognizing your heavenly Father's superior love and knowledge and then allowing Him to show you how to use the bike. Some protest and say they would have to give up many freedoms to obey such a re-strictive Father, but this is not so. In the short term you my feel limited by the Father's vision for your bicycle, but once you learn to ride you will have many times as much freedom as before, because now you can travel great distances and explore the world your Father has given to you. True freedom is found in submission to the Creator and when you deny Him, even while sighting freedom as your reason, you are only becoming more bound in your own cage.

Anyway, this idea also helped me to form a new thought as to why God let man fall. If God is all-knowing and all-powerful, He would have known before He created man that man would fail. So, He was able to see the future and stop it from happening if He wanted to, but

He did not. Now, without questioning if God is all-powerful or all-knowing, two attributes which are very powerfully attested to by the mere existence of the universe, how could I reconcile God's knowledge of the future and His goodness in a way that allows for the fall of man? God must have wanted man to fall, or at least He must have wanted to allow falling as an option. Why would this be?

Anyway, I have written far too much at this point, I must go. I will think about this and write again tomorrow.

In Christ,

Emily

The signature rung in Nathan's head. *Emily. Emily. Emily,* Nathan thought, again and again, trying to jog some sort of memory he was not sure was even there. After several minutes, Nathan looked at the driver and asked,

"Who is Emily?"

"Well, she is the girl I have been talking about, friend; I can't imagine I've gone all this time without saying her name."

"You have."

"Yes, well, I guess I have. Very well, her name is Emily. Now you know. Her name is of no consequence to you, though. I only mean to tell you my story, after all."

Nathan looked back at the letter and ran his fingers over the words. This letter meant something to him, but he still did not know what.

"She's a bright one, isn't she? I told you she was perceptive, but she wasn't kidding when she said she struggled to be heard. I remember some of our fiercest arguments, and in many of them, she was completely right. But it didn't matter. I could run circles around her with my many words and I'd overwhelm her. I always won the argument in the short term, but after a few hours, she'd come right back with a whole new lot of arguments she intended to try out. She sure did like to test my intellect."

"Did you ever tell her you were wrong?"

The man gave a full-throated laugh, throwing his head back and striking his thigh.

"Of course, but it always proved to be more difficult than just insisting I was correct. You see, admitting defeat was difficult, but admitting she was right was a whole different thing! Now, I could stand to lose, but I could not let her win."

"Isn't that—well, mean?"

"Yes, of course."

Nathan felt pains of compassion for Emily. She clearly had liked this man more than he knew, yet he seemed to have treated her as nothing more than a whetstone by which he sharpened his intellect. Nathan had believed his driver was self-righteous and arrogant, but he was beginning to see perhaps this man's joy was real. After all, he was able to admit his faults and still maintain his joy. *It is true*, Nathan thought, *this driver is overbearing, presumptuous, and at times rude, but he is genuine. The driver truly believes all he has done has been forgiven, but why should that free him from guilt? Why should Emily suffer and this man be free?* Nathan then asked the driver,

"If you are the one who hurt her, why do you seem so gleeful?"

"Forgiveness. It's sweet, and it makes you happy."

"You're referring to the girl, the one you wronged?"

"Yes of course, but it's even better than that. The one I truly wronged also forgave me."

"I fail to see who else you wronged in this situation; are you referring to some other, greater sin?"

"No, I am referring to my Creator."

Here we go again, Nathan thought. *Just when he starts to make sense, he returns to this incoherent dribble about God.* Despite his annoyance at the driver's insistence on preaching at him, Nathan had become interested in the story. The girl, Emily, seemed to him a very interesting character, and he could not shake the feeling that she was important to him in some greater way.

Nathan, ignoring the driver's attempt to talk about Jesus, asked, "What's with these letters? Why do they move as you read them?"

"I call those side effects," the driver said, nodding his head. "But I can assure you, I see the same thing when I read them. I will warn you though, each of the six letters will have various effects on you. I encourage you to read along, but I will not force you." The man paused and took a deep, introspective breath. "This one is interesting, though. I believe this caused me to see living words."

How could this old man force me to do anything, let alone read these letters? Nathan asked himself. "I will read on because *I* want to—wait, what do you mean living words?"

"Before, I saw words as weapons. I used them to get what I wanted, and it didn't matter much to me if I was being honest, or if the words had true meanings. I could turn each and every word into a blade to carve free my chunk of flesh with no regard for others. Now, I see words differently. I see they have a purpose, and it is for me to use them with meaning."

Nathan was still confused by the driver's response, but he decided to change the subject.

"I have one more question."

"Alright." The driver nodded as if to say, go on.

"You said she sent you hundreds of letters, but here you only have six, why is that?"

"These six letters tell our story. These six are important for more than just communication between myself and Emily, but I am sure your question will be answered more fully in time."

For a moment, Nathan thought he saw a man standing on the side of the road beckoning to him, but as the car drove past the spot where he thought he saw him, the man had vanished. Nathan turned his gaze upon the unopened envelope in his hands, and at that moment resolved in his heart that he would read all six letters.

Four

Beech Tree

Nathan turned the letter over in his hand and began to pick at the binding on the back of the envelope. It had been opened before, and was resealed by humidity. Nathan acted with caution, trying not to tear the envelope because its contents were obviously important to the driver. After several minutes of Nathan working on the seal, the driver noticed him struggling.

"Give it here."

Nathan handed him the envelope. With one swift motion, the driver placed the edge of the envelope in his mouth and tore it off. He pulled the letter out and placed it on top of the envelope and handed it back to Nathan.

"Thank you," said Nathan.

Setting aside the letter for a moment, Nathan admired the drawing on the front of the envelope. There was a large beech tree with limbs that stretched off the ends of the paper. It was drawn with the same black ink as the last picture, but this one was drawn with much more detail. Nathan reached for the letter. Upon closer examination, he noticed the driver had not just torn the envelope but had also taken the very top of the letter off. To add to Nathan's growing frustration, the paper that contained the driver's name sat in the lap of the driver. Apprehensive to bother him, Nathan suppressed his curiosity and began to read.

This is the 31st letter I have sent you. I am convinced at this point you are not receiving my letters, but I will continue to include the introduction I have placed in all the rest.

I have decided to write to you. I did not know where to send these letters, and so I have sent them to your childhood home where, I believe, your Mother and Father still live. I have sent them there in hopes they will be forwarded to you, wherever you are. If you have not gotten the others, but for some reason, you got this one, do not be worried, I have made copies of all the rest and I can give them all to you when you return.

Now, onto more important business. I do not mean to repeat myself, but do you remember in the first letter when I asked why God would have wanted the fall to happen? Well, I have addressed this question a few times already, and so I do not mean to rehash it, but the answer seems so obvious to me now. It's as if my will is coming in contact with His. Does that make sense, or am I blaspheming? You know how I worry about purveying a false notion of God.

Maybe I should explain further. I believe God allowed the fall to happen so man would have the real choice between God and not God, or as I said in the first letter, good and evil. God allowed the option of evil so those who chose Him would be making a real choice, and not just producing an output of a function God had rigged. I think God cares about free will. I think He cares so much that He allowed His son to die, at least in part, to afford it to us. This is all, of course, very profound and academic stuff only an intellectual such as myself could understand, don't you think? I hope you can read my tone; I am not serious, but this is the point I am trying to make. I am not an intellectual. I am a common woman. I do not mean I am normal, but common. It seems to me that knowledge of our God is obtainable to anyone who seeks it. I strove to know God and His word and I am learning more about it, but more than that, it makes sense now. I look back at what I learned as I wrote my letters to you, and I cannot for the life of me figure out how I did not see it before. It's as if my entire perspective has shifted to be His perspective now. I still have questions, sure, but now it's no longer about whether the base of it is true, and instead, a desire to know Him more. Isn't that wonderful! I am starting to understand why we are called Christians. "Little Christs" is what it means, and now, I am more proud than ever to be associated with that title. No combinations of syllables could be sweeter to my ears than to hear myself associated with Him.

I almost forgot—before I get too far in the letter, did you notice what was on the cover of this envelope? It's a beech tree. *Fagus grandifolia.* We found it as we explored with your brother. Do you remember what we discussed while we sat in its branches? I called you an arrogant fool. Do you remember that? I suppose I was not always the kindest to you, but at the time, I felt you deserved it. You sat in that tree and dared *to say all other religions were wrong. This was before I had converted, and I felt personally affronted by this statement and so, I pointed out you could not possibly know better than everyone else because you were such an impossible fool. You barely heard me, I think, and you kept right along, telling all about how the Christian text is reliable and this and that and whatever else. I would like to tell you my perspective now, and I fear I may give credence to the arrogant statement you made in that Fagus grandifolia. I may even repeat some of your points, but please, do be gracious with me.*

I had always thought of the Bible as one book written by God. I thought to myself, did the Jewish people find this book with leather binding written in the king's English, just laying on a rock somewhere? Of course, this was not a good argument, but to my mind, it was all I needed to dismiss the Bible as absurd. Of course, there were many more reasons to dismiss the Bible, such as science, the hypocrisy of the Church, and the altogether fantastic nature of the events it records. None of these may be altogether good reasons to reject Christianity, but they remain reasons that sat in my mind. To discuss these objections, I realized I needed to understand what the Bible was. Now, you remember the rest, the Bible is a reliable collection of historical documents telling a cohesive story about the creation, fall, and redemption of mankind. I do not feel I need to describe every step at this time; perhaps later. The aspect of all this that struck me recently was not the reliability of the Bible, though it is reliable, but the difficulties I faced when trying to believe other religions.

I'll start with atheism. Atheism is the belief that there is no god. No god. None at all. (The thoughts I am about to write are not completely my own, they consist of some hodgepodge of all the books I have read on this matter. C.S. Lewis was my inspiration for this particular thought.) For me to believe atheism, I needed to believe almost every person on earth since the beginning of human history has been fundamentally wrong about one of the most essential and basic assumptions of human existence. It felt supremely arrogant to reject God outright when I put it that way, but then, I thought of the sky. Yes, it was true almost every person since the beginning of recorded history believed there was a God, but a good number of them also believed the earth was flat and the sun traveled around the Earth, and I rejected those notions without a twinge of guilt. How was it that I was comfortable rejecting the world's belief on one account, but not the other? I gave this a lot of thought, and I concluded that science cannot study God.

Science is not an all-encompassing force that can explain everything. I'll give you one easy example: History. Science cannot explain history. Allow me to explain, not for your sake, but my own, as I am sure you have already understood my point. Science is a method to ascertain what is true, and let me also say it is quite good at accomplishing this task. Science is confined, though, by what we call the scientific process. Science can only test things that can be repeated, observed, and measured. History obviously can't be repeated, and even if it could, repeating an event would not prove in any way it had happened previously. For example, I recently heard a story of a man who was convinced Native Americans had somehow traveled to the

Malaysian Islands. The good people of Malaysia had sweet potatoes that originated in South America, so there was only one explanation in this man's mind—they must have come across the ocean. So, he went to South America and built a boat. He only used products available to the people who lived there at the time when they supposedly sailed the Pacific. Then, he sailed across the ocean. For him, and many of his supporters, he proved this is what happened: the Native Americans had sailed the Pacific Ocean. But, did he really prove it? No, of course not; just because something can happen does not in any way mean it did happen. He certainly proved it was possible, but he supplied no motive for these people to have done such a task. They were by all accounts completely unaware anything lied over the ocean in the first place. You would have to believe these intelligent people got in a boat, grabbed some sweet potatoes, and voyaged into what, at best, was the unknown, but to them must have seemed like certain death. If I repeat a historical event, it does not prove it has happened, and so, all of that to say science is limited in its scope.

This means if something is noncorporeal, then science cannot study it, at least not yet. So, while there is ample evidence the Earth is a sphere and it orbits the sun, the statement that God is dead cannot be scientifically verified. So, we must ask ourselves, why did almost all of mankind believe there must be a God? It is a good question, and not one that can be easily brushed away with a claim that everyone before us were just ignorant and foolish. In fact, to say such a thing would be the height of arrogant ignorance on our part.

Putting aside atheism for the moment, I began to feel all religions could be separated into two categories: religions founded on the testimony of one man, and religions founded on the testimony of many. This pretty much breaks down into Judaism and Christianity on one side, and all other religions on the opposite side. Islam was a religion given to the prophet Muhammad by Allah, Mormonism was a religion given to Joseph Smith by the archangel Gabriel, and even Buddhism was founded on the testimony of Buddha's journey to find enlightenment. I have, of course, left many religious out of this dichotomy for the sake of brevity. The Bible seemed altogether different. It was not a book, but a collection of books, written by over 40 different authors over a time spanning around 1500 years. Now, of course, this does not mean Christianity is true and all other religions are false, but this simple fact made Christianity seem all the more plausible to me.

Anyway, I believe I have written too much, as my hand has begun to ache again. I will put this letter in the mail tomorrow because I've already sent one today. I hope to see you soon.

In Christ,

Emily

As Nathan looked up from the letter, everything in his vision became purple. He wiped his eyes again and again, but the world remained purple.

"You see the world differently now, don't you?"

"Everything is purple."

"Indeed, you will get used to it. As I said earlier, every letter has a side effect, and this one happens to dress the world like royalty."

"Will it ever go away?" Nathan asked with a twinge of fear in his voice. "I'm not quite sure I want to see everything this way forever. Perhaps for a time, but not indefinitely."

"And why not? Before you go on about how you want the freedom to choose and all that, look." The driver bent down and pulled a picture from the floor of the car. He held it up and so Nathan could make out an image of two little boys playing with toy swords. "Do you see this differently, then?"

Nathan, now annoyed that this man seemed to have permanently altered his ability to see, immediately responded, "There is no difference in the subject matter of the image, of course. It was two little boys playing toy swords before, and it is now. The only thing that's changed is the color of the image, as we already discussed. Why do you insist on asking me a nonsensical question?" The man did not answer and he held the image steadily in Nathan's view. "I asked you a question. Can't you hear me?" The driver did not move or hint that he had heard Nathan's words. So, Nathan tried again, this time in a louder voice. "Excuse me sir, but it seems you have permanently changed my vision to purple and I'd like an explanation at once."

This time, the driver responded. "Look."

The driver shook the picture still raised by his right hand. Then, from the corner of his eye, he saw the face of one of the boys. He was crying. Nathan did not see that at first. He had thought the two boys were just having a glad time smacking one another over the head with these wooden swords, but no, one of them was crying. Nathan leaned forward and ripped the picture from the driver's hand. The driver did not flinch. He only returned his hand to the wheel. Nathan peered closely at the boy's face. There were bruises, and Nathan had not seen them before. Nathan felt something new. He did not only know the boy was in pain, but he felt the marks were not just an affront to not just him, but to something greater. Nathan's heart ached for the world to be set right.

"Have I ever seen this image before?"

The driver nodded.

"Did I not see that one boy was in pain before? Is that the difference?" The driver did not answer the question, and this gave Nathan pause. He thought, *Yes, I had seen the image before, and I remembered the pain in the child's face, so what was different now?* "Well, I guess I did not see the severity of the thing before. Is that what you are trying to tell me? Why do you have such a horrid picture in your car anyway?" Nathan said, gesturing to the image.

The driver grinned, "So it happened to you, too?"

"What happened to me? What are you blathering on about?"

"You see value. It is easy to live life in the dark. If you cannot see suffering, how can it upset you? Once the world was purple though, everything was illuminated. It was something like being in a dark room for a while and then abruptly having the lights turned on. My eyes stung, my head ached, and I was not prepared for what I would see. Before, I saw people as means by which I could gain benefit, but after; I began to see they meant something all on their own. Value was not a trait that I imparted upon those in my life, but instead it was an immutable quality.

More than that, I saw they had value that came from God. This value that God placed in the world caused me great pain to see. Before, it was easy enough to only bother over my own problems. 'Mind your own business' was my motto and it kept me happy in a shallow sense. In some cases, keeping to myself may have been the right thing to do, but many other times it was an excuse to turn a blind eye to situations where I was needed. Now, suffering is not only an affront against me, but against God. It's as if the whole of existence is crying out for God to set things straight and I along with it. Before, when you looked at that picture, you saw two young boys playing. You didn't care if one was crying, because after all, that is what young children do; but now, you see the value in even the emotion in the young boy's face. It is a silly example of how things have changed, but it's a useful demonstration. You wish this boy would not have to experience this pain, not for your sake, but his. Before you feared tears because they showed weakness, but now tears represent the brokenness of this world, a brokenness we both ache will be set right one day."

Nathan, insulted by the driver's insistence he had been changed by this letter, took to accusing him. "What do you know about it? For all you know, this picture struck me with emotions too deep for words—did you ever think of that? *You* may have been an ill-minded sociopath before you saw the world in purple, but I certainly was not."

"That is your picture."

"What do you mean? It was in your car, and I am certainly not one of the children in the image."

"Look at it again."

Nathan looked down and was at once aware that the picture was inside of a wallet. Nathan turned the fold of the wallet over and saw the license inside was his. "This is my wallet?"

"Yes, my friend, you tried to hand it to me when you got into the car, but it fell out of your frozen hands and landed at my feet."

"Yes, I remember now, but I cannot remember who is in this photograph."

"It's alright, I am sure this lapse in memory serves some function; you will remember later."

The assurance of the driver did not serve to comfort Nathan. He was now even more distrusting of the driver and confused by the whole situation he found himself in.

"What is going on?" Nathan asked with a whimper. "I am tired of this game. Why won't you tell me?"

"Read the next letter. I promise you this: my story is worth your time," said the driver, ignoring his passenger's pleas.

Nathan looked down at the letters sitting on his lap. He picked up the third one, and this time, he ripped the envelope himself.

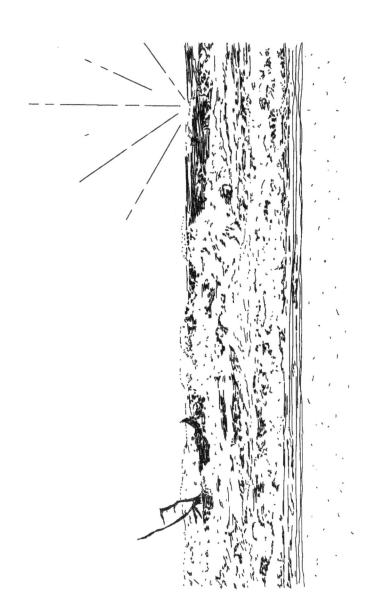

Five

A Great Expanse

Nathan hesitated to pull the letter from its envelope. The last side effect was worse than he had expected, and despite his earlier resolution to continue reading, he wondered if it was worth the risk of opening the remaining letters. *Looking at the picture on the front couldn't hurt*, he assured himself. The picture was of an ocean. There was a large piece of driftwood amid the waves. The picture was drawn by the same pen as the rest, but this image appeared different to Nathan. He stared intently at the image and became convinced the drawing was moving. He watched the waves crash down on the beach as the driftwood rose and lowered in time. Drawn in the distance, far across the ocean, was an island, where emanated a brilliant light. Nathan was immediately drawn to it, but at times, the waves rose so high they obstructed the view of the island, and each time it was obscured, he shook the image, hoping to send the waves back so he could see the island again. He felt his eyes being drawn to the island so strongly he began to fear he would not be able to look away. The beauty of the image was breathtaking, and he couldn't help but feel something was changing inside of him the more he looked. *What was this place?* he thought. His curiosity once more overwhelmed his apprehension to read the letter. Upon pulling it from the envelope, he noticed the name at the top was hidden from his mind, but this time, it didn't bother him because his purpose was to learn of the island. The letter opened in the same way as the previous one:

Dear ----

Well, it's a little more than a month now after you've left, and since I began to write to you. I did not know where to send these letters, and so I have sent them to your childhood home where, I believe, your Mother and Father still live. I have sent them there in hopes they will be forwarded to you, wherever you are. However, if you have not gotten the others, but for some reason you got this one, do not be worried, I have made copies of all the rest and I can give them all to you when you return.

I would like to discuss the image on the front of this envelope. You may have been confused when you saw it since all my previous letters to you displayed some image of a place we both visited, and as you undoubtedly know, we have never gone to the beach. Then why did I draw it? Well, that is a funny story. I was walking in the supermarket when I got into a little tiff with a man who was buying cereal. When he saw me, he snarled at me. I was confused, I had done nothing to this man and there were plenty of Cheerios to go around, and so

I assumed that I had misinterpreted this man's look. I proceeded right along and grabbed myself a box of cereal, and would you believe this man knocked the box out of my hand?

Now, I will describe this man to you only to provide a full perspective of the situation, not because I think it has any bearing on his behavior, though it may have. This man was about six feet tall with long black hair. He had such a pot belly that it almost appeared he was pregnant. He wore tight black jeans, a white V-neck top, and boots that came up halfway to his knees. He had a dog collar around his neck and, from what I could tell, he normally had a soft, warm face. Though, in this instance, he was clearly quite mad at me.

I must give you a few more details of the situation for you to understand fully. His name, as I learned later, was Arthur. Arthur and I both passed a man standing outside the grocery store on our way in. He was yelling about gay people, promiscuous women, and even people who wear tight pants. Of course, he was saying they were all destined for a fiery demise, you know how these things go. Well, when I walked by this man, I greeted him with a very courteous 'good day,' inquired about his name, and politely asked the man if he could please step down from his box and have a meal with me. Of course, I was not interested in dating the man, far from it, but I guess he did not know that, and neither did the onlookers. Much to my delight, the man said yes and proceeded to sit down on his box and wait for me to finish my shopping. I am sure you know why I did this. I wanted to speak to the man about his methods of "evangelism," but if I debated with him right there, he'd merely shout over me, and you know how that goes. So, I intended to argue with him over the pretense of dinner. Well, Arthur saw me ask the man out to eat and, I can only assume, he believed I had done so because I agreed with the man. So, when Arthur, a gay man, saw me reaching for the Cheerios, his rage boiled over, and he struck them from my hand. Of course, Arthur's behavior was reprehensible; even if I agreed with the man outside, it would not justify this action. But in a moment of supernatural (I say supernatural because it was His will, not mine) clarity, I asked Arthur if I could pay for his groceries. Arthur looked at me, stupefied, and he began to cry. It turns out Arthur was a musician, and that day he was making the very painful choice between eating and paying his rent. Of course, being a musician for a living, he brought this situation on himself to a degree, but regardless, I was feeling quite charitable and so I paid for his groceries. Before you become indignant at my previous comment, I am only poking fun at a friend. Please forgive my grim sense of humor. Anyway, Arthur followed me out of the store. On my way out, I told the man whom I had previously asked to a meal to call me for a dinner later that night. I gave the man my number, and Arthur and I left together.

Now, you may be thinking that this is a fantastic story, and it has literally nothing to do with a beach. You would be right on the first account; I can't quite believe it myself! But on the second, you would be wrong. You see, once we had gotten in my car, Arthur asked me, "Why do you want to date that horrid Christian man, anyway?" I laughed and I said to him, "Is that what you think? I can assure you, I have no more desire to date that man than I do to scrub toilets at the local public restroom." Arthur was confused, so I explained. I had asked the man to dinner because I wanted to discuss the reasons for his yelling and it would not hurt that I'd get a free meal out of the whole thing. "So, you don't agree with him, then?" Arthur asked me, momentarily relieved. I said, "No, I do agree with him, I only think his list ought to be much longer." Arthur looked at me and gasped, but I went right on explaining. "That list should include words like liars, cheaters, people who get wrongly divorced, hypocrites, those who are prideful, idolatrous, and anyone who has ever lusted. Honestly, I cannot even think of a single person who does not belong on that list." Arthur, now less confused and more curious, asked, "Well if everyone is going to Hell, according to you, why shouldn't we all just do whatever we want anyway?" So, I went right on explaining the Gospel, that we all are sinners who deserve Hell, and you know all the rest. I cannot say Arthur left my house and became baptized that very same day, but I can say this: he heard a Christian tell him the truth for once, and I feel like that is something.

The thing that struck me about the whole circumstance is the reality of how lost we really are. Even this man who is preaching the reality of sin was so lost that he thought angering people was a good way to win them for Christ. I feel like we are all on a beach of a deserted island. The waves are crashing down on the shore and we have nothing to fashion a boat from. We all see, at one time or another, an island off in the distance. There is light coming from it, and sometimes we can even hear the sound of joy emanating from its center. Some people try to swim there and realize it is too far, and so they come back. Others are convinced the island is nothing more than an illusion produced by our lack of good food and water. Still, others wander the beach, studying the sand, trying to find some clue proving the island is real. There is no way for any of us to get from the shore to that island. Then, a man from the island comes by on a very large boat. He tells us he is going back to the island, and anyone can come if they choose. Some stubbornly say they shall find their own way to the island and this man's help is very much not welcome. Others tell the man he is insane, and there is, in fact, no island at all! Even if there is one, they add, there is no way to know about it. They must have forgotten the man was on a boat, but regardless, they return to fuddling about in the sand. Still, others tell the boat captain they are far too comfortable on the beach. On the shore, they are in control of their lives, they can bask in the sun, and they can even eat a fish now and again. To them, giving all that up just to see some lousy island was not something they were prepared to do. Of course, there are many more reasons a person will reject the captain's invitation, but some say, "I have nothing to pay you with." The captain calls back, "I want nothing from you." They then say, "But I cannot get to you; the waves are too strong." So, the captain leaps from the boat, wades through the waves, feeling every sting of the ice-cold water on his skin, every fear and temptation we have ever had to face on that shore. The captain reaches his hand out to us, we take it, and he carries us on his shoulders all the way back to the boat.

This is what He did for us: isn't it wonderful? Doesn't it make you just want to scream into your pillow? This story could not be greater, it could not be truer, it could not be more real. As I reflected on this, I realized something else about religion. Again, I want to split all religions into two categories: one category is all religions teaching what one must do to atone for their mistakes (they teach you how to swim) and the other category is made up of religions of grace (they teach you to get on the boat). I believe that by doing this, I have separated every religion in the world from only Christianity. Every religion teaches us how to swim, how to bridge the great expanse existing between us and God. Some religions teach fasts, pilgrimages, and prayers as a means of salvation, but, while Christianity has those things, they are not means of salvation for us. Christians are first saved by no merit of their own, just fully by grace, and then because of that grace, are inspired to know more of the God who saved them and to obey His will.

This response just seems truer to me than all the rest. How could a bunch of fasts pay God back for the things I have done wrong anyway? We call the fasts obedience, don't we? But we only perform a few fasts a year. Do these few acts of obedience in any way compare to the amount of disobedience I showed in that very same year? Even if they did, I still fail to see how they would atone for what I had done wrong. Allow me to explain; let's say at the end of my life, 51% of my life was spent in obedience, and only 49% was spent in disobedience. This would be a feat I am sure only great saints could hope to achieve. Regardless, let's say I did it. Does the mere fact that 51 is larger than 49 in any way account or make up for the fact that I still spent 49% of my life in disobedience? Do I not still deserve great punishment for disobeying that much? Furthermore, God does not demand 'good enough.' He demands perfection. He demands 100% of my life, and if this is so, then the only way for us to get to 100% is for God to give us righteousness that is not ours. This righteousness also cannot be something we earn, but it must be a free gift. Otherwise, it would be like buying a million dollars for six cents, the pennies being all your good works and a million dollars being perfection. Only an idiot or a loving father would make such a trade, and it is far more likely the father would reject your six pennies on account of he really just was giving you a million dollars, and it was not a trade at all. It seems to me only grace can make sense of how sinful we are, and how good God is.

Oh, and I'd wager you are wondering about that man at the grocery store and how my dinner went with him. Well, let me just say he was not altogether keen on the fact that I showed up wearing tight pants. In hindsight, it was not the wisest and most gracious thing for me to do, but it got the conversation going from the start. Unfortunately, I cannot say his heart was changed, but I can say I didn't back down, and he spoke to me very kindly. Perhaps I planted a seed, and maybe he will use his very evident passion for evangelism in a different way in the future.

Well, that is all I have to say for now. I will place this letter in the mail on Monday, as today is Saturday and I cannot get to the post office today. I hope you are doing fine and this letter will find you soon.

In Christ,

Emily

Nathan sat the letter down and began to wait for the side effect to set in. He wondered what it would be this time. *A permanent ringing in the ears? A smell of feet everywhere I go? Perhaps*

I'll sprout a third arm from my chest. After a few moments, he did not notice any change. As Nathan waited to learn his fate, he allowed his mind to wander. He began to think of the island Emily had discussed. What had she meant? The questions he had before he began to read had not yet been fully answered. He knew the island was a metaphor, but he couldn't shake the feeling that it was also real. As Nathan waited, he tried to remember where he was going, his mother's name, and if he had anything to pay the driver with. A cloud seemed to linger over these memories, making them impossible to access; after minutes of trying, he had enough and turned his attention back to the driver.

"I don't feel any different."

"Yes, I thought the same thing after I read that letter."

"What was the change you experienced?"

"This is a subtle one. It's not quite as in-your-face as a purple world was, but I believe this is the one where my ears grew."

"Your ears grew?" Nathan asked incredulously. He leaned forward to see for himself. Sure enough, this man had the largest ears he had ever seen. "Why did your ears grow?"

"After reading that letter, I knew I needed to hear other people more. My ears grew so I could listen better. My mouth did not shrink, though, and I think that is important to say. It's not that I needed to speak less, it was only that I needed to listen more. I am still allowed, even encouraged, to share my opinions with anyone who will listen, but I also needed to hear theirs, and more than that, I needed to hear *them.*"

"If you talk the same amount and listen more, well, that's just a recipe for long conversations, don't you think?"

"Of course. That is just the point, you see. I didn't care before what people thought. They either agreed with me or they were wrong. So, either way, what would be the point in listening? Well, I now value people over the point. In fact, now, they are the point."

"Oh, yes, well, I just hope my ears don't look like that."

"It is not altogether terrible. Just wear a very large hat."

"What did she mean by the island? Is it real?"

"That is a question you will have to answer, my friend, but I believe the letters may be of some use."

"She said it's free to go there, is that so?"

"In a way, but also in a way, it costs everything."

"What do you mean? How can a thing be free and yet cost everything?"

"Well, imagine you have been loaned a million dollars, and you get yourself into massive debt. Okay?"

"Okay."

"So, the man who loaned you the money asks for you to pay back what you owe, and you cannot pay him because you have spent all of it and have nothing. Okay?"

"Alright."

"The man offers you a deal. He will pay your debt and absorb the one-million-dollar loss only if you are willing to let him be the master of your life."

"Well, that sounds cruel. Doesn't it sound that way to you?"

"Yes, I think it does, especially in the context of a wealthy businessman who is just as flawed as we are. The idea I am trying to communicate is that your life was given to you, and once you had it, you misused it. Now, the God who gave it to you loves you dearly and wants to see everything set right again, so He offers you a deal. He will pay for everything, but He wants you to love Him This seems to be a fairly easy deal to make. Why wouldn't you love someone who had paid all your debts? The problem is love, if you mean the feeling, cannot be conjured. I cannot choose to love God in this way anymore then I can choose to love a gifted pair of hideous shoes. What I can choose is to submit to His love. I can say to God, 'I need you, I know that, but I do not know you, so how could I love you? I want to know you. Help me to know you.' And in that sentence, when said truly, you will render to God a piece of yourself. A piece that He will use to recreate you from top to bottom. He will reveal Himself more and more and love is all that can come from that. Whether love or obedience comes first is a secondary issue; if one is truly there, the other is soon to follow, or perhaps, they are inseparable. Now, this is not a deal to be bartered. You cannot choose to fake it because He cannot be tricked. In this way, my analogy is flawed. God will take your debts and burdens. He just wants you to willingly be His, but you must want that, too. You must yourself, want to be His."

"What if I want Him to pay my debt, but I do not love him?"

"There may be many reasons to give your life to Him. Some do because of fear, others out of self-interest, and others because they love Him. One thing is true about them all: if they truly give their lives to Him, they will love Him in the end."

"You mean if someone says to God, 'I do not love you, but I sure do not want to go to Hell, will you take me?' He would take that person?"

"I do not pretend to understand the ways of God fully and I do not want to speak for Him, but I will say what I can. I believe if that person is truly interested in having his sins paid for, believes Christ can do it, and wants God to be his God, then I can't imagine why God would not forgive his sins. I do want to say again though, everyone who chooses Him loves Him in the end."

"Why should that be so?"

"At first, you will accept Him with only a partial picture of who He is. You may see Him as merely life insurance instead of a loving father. This kind of thinking may lead to the very situation you described previously. As you walk alongside Him, your image of Him cannot help but grow to be fuller. Once you have a full image of God, there is no other response a human could muster other than the deepest and most transcendent love man can offer. If we do not love Him, it is because we do not know Him. If we do not know Him, it is because we do not want to."

Nathan closed his eyes and tried to conjure a feeling of love. He remembered he had felt love before, but he could not recall the object of it and so he thought about love itself. Nathan could not remember anything. Every time he was close to some memory or another, the island filled his mind. After a few moments, Nathan directed his love toward what he believed the island to be. As Nathan closed his eyes and began to feel love again, his ears grew. *The driver was right, it was not altogether terrible,* Nathan thought.

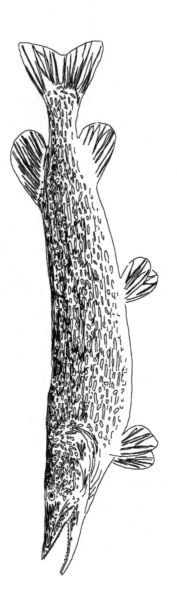

Six

The Northern Pike

As Nathan's ears grew, he became more aware of his surroundings. His world was larger and many new aspects of life availed themselves to him. He heard small pieces of asphalt being tossed against the floor of the car, he heard the breathing of the driver (it was now much more even and calm than before), and he heard birds singing.

"Birds?" Nathan exclaimed to the driver.

"I hear them too."

"Were they always there?" Nathan asked with boyish excitement.

"Yes, we move much too fast to hear them most of the time, though."

"It's funny. A thing as simple as the sound of birds was going on all around us, but I was unable to hear it. Have you ever heard anything quite as wonderful as this?"

"Yes."

"What was it?"

"That question should be answered in the next letter, my friend."

"You know you could just tell me. What if I'm tired of reading these letters?"

"I certainly hope that is not the case."

Nathan let out a quick sharp sigh to let the driver know he was annoyed and went back to experiencing the world about him. Words had meaning, the world was purple, and he could hear. He marveled at his own existence.

Nathan turned to look in the distance, and he saw a man walking with his head bent over, peering at the ground in front of him. He had more strength in his shoulders than any man he had seen before, but yet, he seemed heavy in some capacity; as if he carried some great burden. Nathan could not quite determine what gave him this thought, but he was sure of it.

"Are you going to stop for this man? He will freeze!"

"No. He'll meet us there."

"How could he meet us there if he freezes to death?" Nathan pressed the driver. The car flew passed the man. He did not look up.

"We must go back. He will freeze!"

"He'll be okay, I assure you."

"How could you possibly know that? Turn this car around!"

"Please, calm down. I know this man well. He'll be fine." For some reason, this assurance comforted Nathan, though he did not know why. "Look at the fifth letter."

Nathan looked down, and within seconds he had all but forgotten about the man he had just seen. On the front of the envelope was depicted a large fish. "What is this fish?"

"It is a Northern Pike," the driver said with such joy that he now sounded to be only a few years older than Nathan.

"Why is it on here? Or—I suppose I ought to just read the letter."

The driver nodded with a grin across his face that warmed Nathan's heart a little. He looked back to the envelope and watched the fish wriggle back and forth as if it were swimming through a lake. The fish was large and had teeth. Each tooth was curved backward, presumably to keep anything that it swallowed from trying to escape certain death. The fish was long and slender, with small spots on its back and head. It was so detailed that it almost seemed to be alive. *I wonder if this will bite me?* He slowly and cautiously placed his finger right on the place where the mouth of the fish was drawn. The fish made a quick turning motion and Nathan, startled, withdrew his finger. The driver began to laugh uncontrollably.

"It…It is…a picture." The driver choked out each word in between gasps for air.

Nathan, embarrassed, turned to face the seat, placing his body between the driver and the letter, so the driver could not see what he was doing. The sounds of the driver's laughter began to fade into the background as Nathan, this time delicately, pulled the letter from its sheath and unfolded it. The name at the top of the letter was again invisible to Nathan, but Nathan had grown to accept he would not ever know the driver's name.

Nathan hesitated to pull the letter from its envelope. The last side effect was worse than he had expected, and despite his earlier resolution to continue reading, he wondered if it was worth the risk of opening the remaining letters. *Looking at the picture on the front couldn't hurt,* he assured himself. The picture was of an ocean. There was a large piece of driftwood amid the waves. The picture was drawn by the same pen as the rest, but this image appeared different to Nathan. He stared intently at the image and became convinced the drawing was moving. He watched the waves crash down on the beach as the driftwood rose and lowered in time. Drawn in the distance, far across the ocean, was an island, where emanated a brilliant light. Nathan was immediately drawn to it, but at times, the waves rose so high they obstructed the view of the island, and each time it was obscured, he shook the image, hoping to send the waves back so he could see the island again. He felt his eyes being drawn to the island so strongly he began to fear he would not be able to look away. The beauty of the image was breathtaking, and he couldn't help but feel something was changing inside of him the more he looked. *What was this place?* he thought. His curiosity once more overwhelmed his apprehension to read the letter. Upon pulling it from the envelope, he noticed the name at the top was hidden from his mind, but this time, it didn't bother him because his purpose was to learn of the island. The letter opened in the same way as the previous one:

Dear ----

Well, it's a little more than a month now after you've left, and since I began to write to you. I did not know where to send these letters, and so I have sent them to your childhood home where, I believe, your

Mother and Father still live. I have sent them there in hopes they will be forwarded to you, wherever you are. However, if you have not gotten the others, but for some reason you got this one, do not be worried, I have made copies of all the rest and I can give them all to you when you return.

I would like to discuss the image on the front of this envelope. You may have been confused when you saw it since all my previous letters to you displayed some image of a place we both visited, and as you undoubtedly know, we have never gone to the beach. Then why did I draw it? Well, that is a funny story. I was walking in the supermarket when I got into a little tiff with a man who was buying cereal. When he saw me, he snarled at me. I was confused, I had done nothing to this man and there were plenty of Cheerios to go around, and so I assumed that I had misinterpreted this man's look. I proceeded right along and grabbed myself a box of cereal, and would you believe this man knocked the box out of my hand?

Now, I will describe this man to you only to provide a full perspective of the situation, not because I think it has any bearing on his behavior, though it may have. This man was about six feet tall with long black hair. He had such a pot belly that it almost appeared he was pregnant. He wore tight black jeans, a white V-neck top, and boots that came up halfway to his knees. He had a dog collar around his neck and, from what I could tell, he normally had a soft, warm face. Though, in this instance, he was clearly quite mad at me.

I must give you a few more details of the situation for you to understand fully. His name, as I learned later, was Arthur. Arthur and

I both passed a man standing outside the grocery store on our way in. He was yelling about gay people, promiscuous women, and even people who wear tight pants. Of course, he was saying they were all destined for a fiery demise, you know how these things go. Well, when I walked by this man, I greeted him with a very courteous 'good day,' inquired about his name, and politely asked the man if he could please step down from his box and have a meal with me. Of course, I was not interested in dating the man, far from it, but I guess he did not know that, and neither did the onlookers. Much to my delight, the man said yes and proceeded to sit down on his box and wait for me to finish my shopping. I am sure you know why I did this. I wanted to speak to the man about his methods of "evangelism," but if I debated with him right there, he'd merely shout over me, and you know how that goes. So, I intended to argue with him over the pretense of dinner. Well, Arthur saw me ask the man out to eat and, I can only assume, he believed I had done so because I agreed with the man. So, when Arthur, a gay man, saw me reaching for the Cheerios, his rage boiled over, and he struck them from my hand. Of course, Arthur's behavior was reprehensible; even if I agreed with the man outside, it would not justify this action. But in a moment of supernatural (I say supernatural because it was His will, not mine) clarity, I asked Arthur if I could pay for his groceries. Arthur looked at me, stupefied, and he began to cry. It turns out Arthur was a musician, and that day he was making the very painful choice between eating and paying his rent. Of course, being a musician for a living, he brought this situation on himself to a degree, but regardless, I was feeling quite charitable and so I paid for his groceries. Before you become indignant at my previous comment, I am only poking fun at a friend. Please forgive my grim sense of humor. Anyway, Arthur followed me out of the store. On my way out, I told the man whom I had previously asked to a meal to call me for a dinner later that night. I gave the man my number, and Arthur and I left together.

Now, you may be thinking that this is a fantastic story, and it has literally nothing to do with a beach. You would be right on the first account; I can't quite believe it myself! But on the second, you would be wrong. You see, once we had gotten in my car, Arthur asked me, "Why do you want to date that horrid Christian man, anyway?" I laughed and I said to him, "Is that what you think? I can assure you, I have no more desire to date that man than I do to scrub toilets at the local public restroom." Arthur was confused, so I explained. I had asked the man to dinner because I wanted to discuss the reasons for his yelling and it would not hurt that I'd get a free meal out of the whole thing. "So, you don't agree with him, then?" Arthur asked me, momentarily relieved. I said, "No, I do agree with him, I only think his list ought to be much longer." Arthur looked at me and gasped, but I went right on explaining. "That list should include words like liars, cheaters, people who get wrongly divorced, hypocrites, those who are prideful, idolatrous, and anyone who has ever lusted. Honestly, I cannot even think of a single person who does not belong on that list." Arthur, now less confused and more curious, asked, "Well if everyone is going to Hell, according to you, why shouldn't we all just do whatever we want anyway?" So, I went right on explaining the Gospel, that we all are sinners who deserve Hell, and you know all the rest. I cannot say Arthur left my house and became baptized that very same day, but I can say this: he heard a Christian tell him the truth for once, and I feel like that is something.

The thing that struck me about the whole circumstance is the reality of how lost we really are. Even this man who is preaching the reality of sin was so lost that he thought angering people was a good way to win them for Christ. I feel like we are all on a beach of a deserted island. The waves are crashing down on the shore and we have nothing to fashion a boat from. We all see, at one time or another, an island off in the distance. There is light coming from it, and sometimes we can even hear the sound of joy emanating from its center. Some people try to swim there and realize it is too far, and so they come back. Others are convinced the island is nothing more than an illusion produced by our lack of good food and water. Still, others wander the beach, studying the sand, trying to find some clue proving the island is real. There is no way for any of us to get from the shore to that island. Then, a man from the island comes by on a very large boat. He tells us he is going back to the island, and anyone can come if they choose. Some stubbornly say they shall find their own way to the island and this man's help is very much not welcome. Others tell the man he is insane, and there is, in fact, no island at all! Even if there is one, they add, there is no way to know about it. They must have forgotten the man was on a boat, but regardless, they return to fuddling about in the sand. Still, others tell the boat captain they are far too comfortable on the beach. On the shore, they are in control of their lives, they can bask in the sun, and they can even eat a fish now and again. To them, giving all that up just to see some lousy island was not something they were prepared to do. Of course, there are many more reasons a person will reject the captain's invitation, but some say, "I have nothing to pay you with." The captain calls back, "I want nothing from you." They then say, "But I cannot get to you; the waves are too strong." So, the captain leaps from the boat, wades through the waves, feeling every sting of the ice-cold water on his skin, every fear and temptation we have ever had to face on that shore. The captain reaches his hand out to us, we take it, and he carries us on his shoulders all the way back to the boat.

This is what He did for us: isn't it wonderful? Doesn't it make you just want to scream into your pillow? This story could not be greater, it could not be truer, it could not be more real. As I reflected on this, I realized something else about religion. Again, I want to split all religions into two categories: one category is all religions teaching what one must do to atone for their mistakes (they teach you how to swim) and the other category is made up of religions of grace (they teach you to get on the boat). I believe that by doing this, I have separated every religion in the world from only Christianity. Every religion teaches us how to swim, how to bridge the great expanse existing between us and God. Some religions teach fasts, pilgrimages, and prayers as a means of salvation, but, while Christianity has those things, they are not means of salvation for us. Christians are first saved by no merit of their own, just fully by grace, and then because of that grace, are inspired to know more of the God who saved them and to obey His will.

This response just seems truer to me than all the rest. How could a bunch of fasts pay God back for the things I have done wrong any-

way? We call the fasts obedience, don't we? But we only perform a few fasts a year. Do these few acts of obedience in any way compare to the amount of disobedience I showed in that very same year? Even if they did, I still fail to see how they would atone for what I had done wrong. Allow me to explain; let's say at the end of my life, 51% of my life was spent in obedience, and only 49% was spent in disobedience. This would be a feat I am sure only great saints could hope to achieve. Regardless, let's say I did it. Does the mere fact that 51 is larger than 49 in any way account or make up for the fact that I still spent 49% of my life in disobedience? Do I not still deserve great punishment for disobeying that much? Furthermore, God does not demand 'good enough.' He demands perfection. He demands 100% of my life, and if this is so, then the only way for us to get to 100% is for God to give us righteousness that is not ours. This righteousness also cannot be something we earn, but it must be a free gift. Otherwise, it would be like buying a million dollars for six cents, the pennies being all your good works and a million dollars being perfection. Only an idiot or a loving father would make such a trade, and it is far more likely the father would reject your six pennies on account of he really just was giving you a million dollars, and it was not a trade at all. It seems to me only grace can make sense of how sinful we are, and how good God is.

Oh, and I'd wager you are wondering about that man at the grocery store and how my dinner went with him. Well, let me just say he was not altogether keen on the fact that I showed up wearing tight pants. In hindsight, it was not the wisest and most gracious thing for me to do, but it got the conversation going from the start. Unfortunately, I can-

not say his heart was changed, but I can say I didn't back down, and he spoke to me very kindly. Perhaps I planted a seed, and maybe he will use his very evident passion for evangelism in a different way in the future.

Well, that is all I have to say for now. I will place this letter in the mail on Monday, as today is Saturday and I cannot get to the post office today. I hope you are doing fine and this letter will find you soon.

In Christ,

Emily

Nathan sat the letter down and began to wait for the side effect to set in. He wondered what it would be this time. *A permanent ringing in the ears? A smell of feet everywhere I go? Perhaps I'll sprout a third arm from my chest.* After a few moments, he did not notice any change. As Nathan waited to learn his fate, he allowed his mind to wander. He began to think of the island Emily had discussed. What had she meant? The questions he had before he began to read had not yet been fully answered. He knew the island was a metaphor, but he couldn't shake the feeling that it was also real. As Nathan waited, he tried to remember where he was going, his mother's name, and if he had anything to pay the driver with. A cloud seemed to linger over these memories, making them impossible to access; after minutes of trying, he had enough and turned his attention back to the driver.

"I don't feel any different."

"Yes, I thought the same thing after I read that letter."

"What was the change you experienced?"

"This is a subtle one.It's not quite as in-your-face as a purple world was, but I believe this is the one where my ears grew."

"Your ears grew?" Nathan asked incredulously. He leaned forward to see for himself. Sure enough, this man had the largest ears he had ever seen. "Why did your ears grow?"

"After reading that letter, I knew I needed to hear other people more. My ears grew so I could listen better. My mouth did not shrink, though, and I think that is important to say. It's not that I needed to speak less, it was only that I needed to listen more. I am still allowed, even encouraged, to share my opinions with anyone who will listen, but I also needed to hear theirs, and more than that, I needed to hear *them*."

"If you talk the same amount and listen more, well, that's just a recipe for long conversations, don't you think?"

"Of course. That is just the point, you see. I didn't care before what people thought. They either agreed with me or they were wrong. So, either way, what would be the point in listening? Well, I now value people over the point. In fact, now, they are the point."

"Oh, yes, well, I just hope my ears don't look like that."

"It is not altogether terrible. Just wear a very large hat."

"What did she mean by the island? Is it real?"

"That is a question you will have to answer, my friend, but I believe the letters may be of some use."

"She said it's free to go there, is that so?"

"In a way, but also in a way, it costs everything."

"What do you mean? How can a thing be free and yet cost everything?"

"Well, imagine you have been loaned a million dollars, and you get yourself into massive debt. Okay?"

"Okay."

"So, the man who loaned you the money asks for you to pay back what you owe, and you cannot pay him because you have spent all of it and have nothing. Okay?"

"Alright."

"The man offers you a deal. He will pay your debt and absorb the one-million-dollar loss only if you are willing to let him be the master of your life."

"Well, that sounds cruel. Doesn't it sound that way to you?"

"Yes, I think it does, especially in the context of a wealthy businessman who is just as flawed as we are. The idea I am trying to communicate is that your life was given to you, and once you had it, you misused it. Now, the God who gave it to you loves you dearly and wants to see everything set right again, so He offers you a deal. He will pay for everything, but He wants you to love Him This seems to be a fairly easy deal to make. Why wouldn't you love someone who had paid all your debts? The problem is love, if you mean the feeling, cannot be conjured. I cannot choose to love God in this way anymore then I can choose to love a gifted pair of hideous shoes. What I can choose is to submit to His love. I can say to God, 'I need you, I know that, but I do not know you, so how could I love you? I want to know you. Help me to know you.' And in that sentence, when said truly, you will render to God a piece of yourself. A piece that He will use to recreate you from top to bottom. He will reveal Himself more and more and love is all that can come from that. Whether love or obedience comes first is a secondary issue; if one is truly there, the other is soon to follow, or perhaps, they are inseparable. Now, this is not a deal to be bartered. You cannot choose to fake it because He cannot be tricked. In this way, my analogy is flawed. God will take your debts and burdens. He just wants you to willingly be His, but you must want that, too. You must yourself, want to be His."

"What if I want Him to pay my debt, but I do not love him?"

"There may be many reasons to give your life to Him. Some do because of fear, others out of self-interest, and others because they love Him. One thing is true about them all: if they truly give their lives to Him, they will love Him in the end."

"You mean if someone says to God, 'I do not love you, but I sure do not want to go to Hell, will you take me?' He would take that person?"

"I do not pretend to understand the ways of God fully and I do not want to speak for Him, but I will say what I can. I believe if that person is truly interested in having his sins paid for, believes Christ can do it, and wants God to be his God, then I can't imagine why God would not forgive his sins. I do want to say again though, everyone who chooses Him loves Him in the end."

"Why should that be so?"

"At first, you will accept Him with only a partial picture of who He is. You may see Him as merely life insurance instead of a loving father. This kind of thinking may lead to the very situation you described previously. As you walk alongside Him, your image of Him cannot help but grow to be fuller. Once you have a full image of God, there is no other response a human could muster other than the deepest and most transcendent love man can offer. If we do not love Him, it is because we do not know Him. If we do not know Him, it is because we do not want to."

Nathan closed his eyes and tried to conjure a feeling of love. He remembered he had felt love before, but he could not recall the object of it and so he thought about love itself. Nathan could not remember anything. Every time he was close to some memory or another, the island filled his mind. After a few moments, Nathan directed his love toward what he believed the island to be. As Nathan closed his eyes and began to feel love again, his ears grew. *The driver was right, it was not altogether terrible,* Nathan thought.

Nathan placed down the letter and was filled with joy. He wanted to scream, but he contained himself and said, "She is wonderful."

"Yes, she is." The driver said smiling widely. Then the smile slowly slipped from his face and he looked to his lap.

Nathan continued, unaware of the solemn look on the driver's face. "And what's that wonderful smell?"

"That is you, my friend."

"Me?" Nathan asked astonished yet again by the driver's bizarre response.

"You're smelling your joy."

"Joy is an emotion; it doesn't have a fragrance," Nathan countered.

Nathan turned to look out the window and felt dumb for explaining that to the driver. He then began trying to place the sweet smell, but he only saw barren cornfields with a light dusting of snow over them. He did not look for long before the smell quickly turned to a foul odor.

Nathan turned to the driver. "What's changed? Where'd the sweet smell go, and why has this horrid smell replaced it?" he asked while holding his nose between his pointer finger and thumb.

"I apologize, that's my fault."

"Oh, don't worry about it. I'm sorry I mentioned it." Nathan felt embarrassed for pointing out that the man had passed gas, but he also heard something in the driver's voice he had not heard before. It sounded like pain.

"Why are you sad? I thought you'd like this letter the best yet. In this one, she all but tells you she loves you, and she really is something special."

"So, you can smell it." The driver said evading the question.

"Yes, I can," Nathan responded, confused.

"I can say this side effect is perhaps the most useful, especially when it comes to interpreting women." The driver chuckled again and his shoulders did the same odd motion they had done before. Nathan took special notice of it this time, as he felt it was of importance to him.

"What do you mean 'interpreting women?'"

"Congratulations, you can now smell feelings."

"Feelings? What on earth are you babbling about?"

"It's not always wonderful, just try to walk through New York City. You won't get very far before you all but faint from the smells of the bad feelings."

"You mean to say, I am literally smelling bad feelings?"

"Yes, and let me say, good feelings are nothing short of divine and they entirely make up for all the pain you will experience while smelling bad feelings."

"So, the wonderful smell earlier was a good feeling?"

"Yes, and just imagine what it smells like when you have an entire body of people worshiping God truly. It brings you right before the throne of God."

"So, you think this effect is good, then?"

"I think they are all good, but yes, I am especially fond of this one."

"What if I get stuck in an area with only bad feelings?"

"Well, you better start giving those people a reason to feel hope."

Nathan began to feel thankful. He did not know why or for what, but he liked feeling this way and he lingered there with increasing joy welling up inside of him.

Seven

Home

Nathan began to feel something was not quite right about the driver. Of course, before he thought the driver was insane, homeless, and a religious fanatic, but now he wondered if he had gotten all of that quite wrong. Nathan did not believe the driver should be placed in those categories any longer, yet as he learned more of him nothing seemed to make sense. The driver never fulfilled Nathan's expectations. *Could this man be sane? Is it just me who has been the problem this whole drive?* Nathan began to wonder to himself. There was certainly something not right about the driver though, and Nathan could almost smell it. This time, he didn't search for something to discount the driver's intelligence or credibility, because it seemed like the driver was suddenly in pain, and Nathan had met this kind of pain before. He seemed to be in mourning and yet he maintained a joy that penetrated all his actions, even the way he drove his car. Nathan began to feel compassion for the driver. He wanted to know the driver's story for the sake of the driver alone. Nathan wanted to help.

"I want to give people a reason to hope," Nathan said. He was unsure if he had directed this comment to the driver, or if he merely wanted to say it.

"Well, what is your reason to hope?" asked the driver.

Nathan paused for an uncomfortably long time. He looked out of the window and watched the snow fall against the road. As Nathan watched, the snow stopped falling and the sun came out. "The sun!"

The driver pulled the car over and Nathan and the driver both opened their doors, placed one leg out of the car, and shielded their eyes as they looked to where the sun showed itself.

"I don't believe it," said the driver with giddy excitement.

Nathan looked down the long, straight road before him and saw hundreds of cars pulled to the side with people standing and looking to the sky. "Do you feel its warmth?" asked Nathan, as he boiled over with excitement.

All around the two men, the snow on the ground was melting and they watched as green shoots began to spring up from the ground. Only sprouts—it was just the beginning. The driver and Nathan stood in silence but communicated something to each other deeper than any words they could have spoken. They both felt love. Great love. It was more real than anything Nathan had ever experienced. Nathan did not yet know where this love was coming from, but he was certain every person who was standing and watching the sun shine was experiencing the same love. All at once, Nathan became aware of the song playing in the car. He could finally hear its lyrics. A chorus of people began to sing.

> Lord haste the day when my faith shall be sight
> The clouds be rolled back as a scroll
> The trump shall resound
> And the Lord shall descend
> Even so, it is well with my soul.

Nathan joined in the song as he and the driver threw back their heads and sang its lyrics with every ounce of increasing strength they had. Streams of tears fell down Nathan's cheeks. Nathan was unsure if he could have stopped if he wanted to, but he knew he did not want to.

As Nathan and the driver stepped back into the car, Nathan's heart was full, and he felt fully awake. He didn't ever want to go back to sleep.

"How much farther 'till we arrive?"

"I don't know, but I believe we are now closer than we've ever been before."

Nathan looked down at the next letter and placed his eyes upon the picture drawn on the front of the envelope. It was a house. It was not a very impressive house, but it looked happy. There was a large tree filling the yard on the left side of the house. On the right side was a driveway going back to a one-car garage. This picture was simple. It didn't move, and it wasn't the prettiest picture he had yet seen, but Nathan liked it the best.

Nathan carefully peeled the envelope open and before he could read it, the driver said, "May I see it?"

Nathan handed the envelope to the driver and the driver pulled the letter out, reached over to his glove compartment, pulled out a pen, and proceeded to scribble something out. He handed the letter back to Nathan. Nathan looked at the letter, and to his dismay, the driver had scribbled out all but the last letter in the name at the top of the page. *So, it's not that he has merely forgotten to tell me his name, it's that he doesn't want me to know it,* Nathan thought.

"Why don't you want me to know your name?"

"I do, but not yet."

Nathan did not press the issue any further because he thought he heard pain in the driver's voice again. So, Nathan looked down at the letter and began to read.

Dear -----n

Well, it's been two-and-a-half months now since you've been gone and since I began to write to you. Today, I went and met your mother! She had been receiving my letters for some time now, and being that she was also in the dark regarding your whereabouts, she didn't forward them to you. Rest assured, she did not want to open them for fear of invading your privacy and so nothing embarrassing has been revealed to her. After some time, your mother decided to write me back herself. She invited me to your house and so I went and met your parents. They were delightful and they are just as ready for you to come home as I am. I went over early, right around ten, and we got talking for so long I didn't leave until after dinner. We talked, laughed, and your mom even cried. She told me she had kept all the letters in their original envelopes and I did not have to worry because you'll be read-

ing every one upon your arrival home. That was certainly nice to hear. Your mom said you should be coming home any day now. When she said that, I felt the anticipation in the pit of my stomach. I can't wait for you to return home.

Now, this idea of home has become an interesting concept for me. I have felt away from home this entire time you have been gone, even though I have been living in my own house. Now I know people have said before that home is where the heart is, and maybe that Hallmark card slogan has a little more wisdom than I had previously thought. For a brief moment, I thought you were my home. I now realize that is not so. God is my home. "For here we have no lasting city, but we seek the city that is to come." Hebrews 13:14. My home and my hope is in Christ. Does this discount the feeling I have when you're not here? No, I do not believe it does.

I think worship is never accomplished alone. Worship by its nature is the communication of passion, love, and peace between a person and God. You cannot be in worship without communication with God and therefore, you cannot worship alone. Obviously, it is possible to worship something other than God, but in such a case I no longer use the word worship, but idolatry. When someone engages in idolatry, they are taking part in the degradation of that thing and of self. This act is juxtaposed to the act of glorification which emanates from worship. When we worship God, we glorify Him, which means that we are "adding weight." When we worship things other than the Creator, it is not worship at all because we, in fact, drain that thing of its true significance by ignoring its real value, which is found in the Creator.

Now, worship can also be communal between people. Remember when I said love can be created when more people share love truly? Well, I believe worship is similar. When one person worships, God is glorified. When two people worship, God is worshipped even more, and I think instead of a simple addition problem, the glorification increases exponentially. God is glorified when we worship together. The reason I love you is because our love reveals more about God and His love for me, and that causes me to love and worship Him more. Sure, I can worship without other people, and yes, God will be glorified by it, but when I am with you, my worship is compounded by yours and the love existing between us. My home is in Christ, but you seem to live there with me.

I do not know if I have made full sense of this issue, but I know this God is honored by my love for you because He is the true object of that love. Now, I'm sure you are confused, and I will try to explain. I am not in any way suggesting I like you in the way your male brain has no doubt concluded. I love you, yes, but that does not mean I want a relationship or anything of that sort. I only mean I want you to come home so we can continue to explore our love for Christ together.

I also want to share with you one other thing. Have you ever seen four small sparrows chasing a large hawk? I've seen this many times in my life, and each time I have been astounded by it. Why should such a large hawk flee from such tiny birds? Can't a mighty hawk just turn about and then eat every one of its pursuers? I do not pretend to know exactly how these birds work or if there is some great reason why the hawk must flee, but as I watched this happen, just yesterday, I couldn't help but feel just like that hawk. It is not that I fear one sparrow or even two, but if there are fifty, I would certainly fly away. Often in my life a single problem faces me, and I feel as if I can handle it all on my own. Before long though, that single problem turns into many. I become overwhelmed and I want to run. I felt like that hawk when I first began to have questions of Christianity. I saw one problem I could not readily answer on my own, but I did not bother much about it. It was only one problem, after all, and I could face it alone. As I began to look deeper, though, the single problem became many and those problems became many more and I began to fear I was thoroughly inept and incapable of answering so many questions. I felt ready to run.

As I watched the hawk I started to wonder, what if that hawk were not alone? You see, what gave the sparrows their strength was not that they were able to defeat the hawk individually, but that there were many of them. I have never seen a single sparrow chase a hawk because, I imagine if any sparrow had attempted to do so, it would not be chasing that hawk for very long. The sparrows have no true strength alone. So, what if the hawk was also not alone? In the past few months, while you have been gone, I have found myself wondering very frequently about the communal nature of man. I have said community is helpful for love, worship, and now for facing fears and doubts. God did not intend for us to answer every question and doubt on our own and by our own intellect. Christ gave us community; He gave us the Church.

I know you are off somewhere trying to find truth on your own, but I cannot help but feel you have gone to the wrong place. To me, you seem to be a hawk chased by sparrows. I wish you would come home so I and others can help you chase those pesky sparrows away.

Today was a great day and meeting your family could not have been more enjoyable. Your brother was keen to see me again and I think I will be meeting up with him later this week. I have said this before, but I will say it again: come home.

In Christ,

Emily

The letter began to feel warm between Nathan's fingertips. He rubbed it back and forth trying to find the source of the heat. His skin began to stretch and his bones began to creak. Nathan looked down at his hands and they seemed to be growing.

"What is happening?!" Nathan exclaimed.

But this was not only happening to him but to the driver and the car as well. Nathan was growing. The cornfields began to fade from view as if he was taking off in a plane, but as Nathan, the driver, and the car all grew, new surroundings came into focus. Nathan was still in a car, still on a road, still in between cornfields, but now the fields were green with new growth. The cars on the road around him were colorful and vibrant. Bright red farmhouses periodically lined the roadside, and perhaps most notably, the sun shone with great warmth. Nathan rolled down his window and leaned his head outside.

"It's warm outside!" Nathan yelled to the driver.

The driver put back the sunroof and stuck his head out of it.

"What are you doing? You'll crash!" Nathan yelled playfully.

The driver said nothing, but only smiled at Nathan and continued along. Nathan was happy. On the right side of the car was a large lake. The road rose far above the lake and looked out over the water. The driver cut across traffic, drove his car into a rest stop on the right side of the road, and then got out. There was a picnic area and a bench that sat on the edge of a cliff facing the water. The driver went to sit on the bench, so Nathan grabbed the sixth letter and followed him.

"Why are we stopping?"

"We're here."

"What do you mean?"

The man pointed out over the water, and there in the middle of the lake was a large island. Light shone from the island and he could hear festive shouting and songs. Nathan looked at the island and said, "I thought we were going to a funeral."

"In a way you are, friend. It's on that island."

"How do I get there?"

"The ferry will be here soon to pick you up. In the meantime, you can read that sixth letter if you'd like."

"What was the effect from the fifth? I know the whole world changed, but I'm not sure what changed in me."

"Everything changed in you."

Nathan did not know precisely what the driver meant, but he knew exactly what he was trying to communicate. He was a new man. Nathan turned over the letter in his hand while looking over the water.

"There's no going back if I read this letter, is there?"

"No, I do not believe there is."

Nathan knew at that moment he must make a choice. He was not certain what the two options were, but he knew the right one.

Eight

Arboretum

Before Nathan could read the letter, the ferry had come. Nathan and the driver both went down some steps and got onto the boat. Behind them came a man. Nathan was sure it was the same freezing man from earlier who they had passed some miles back. *How had he gotten here too?* Nathan wondered silently. The man walked past Nathan and the driver and entered a room in the center of the ferry. The driver and Nathan sat next to each other on a bench. Over the loudspeaker came the captain's voice.

It was muddled and hard to make out, but Nathan was almost certain it said, "Welcome aboard, it's time to go home."

The ferry shoved off from the dock and Nathan watched as the water turned behind the boat. The island seemed far away to him, but he also worried it was much too close. Nathan wanted to finish hearing the driver's story before he arrived at the island.

"Go on, read it," the driver encouraged Nathan.

"Do you want to hide the name?"

"No."

Nathan slowly drew the letter from the envelope. He unfolded it and looked at the name at the top: "Dear Nathan."

"I don't understand, your name is Nathan too?"

The driver looked uneasy and did not answer Nathan's question, but instead, he said, "Read it."

The envelope was filled with trees, bushes, and flowers of all kinds. Small animals were running between the shrubs and two small children sat in the foreground petting a squirrel. Nathan opened the letter and began to read.

Dear Nathan,

It's only been a few hours since I wrote to you last about meeting your Mother and Father. Once I had finished writing that letter, I wanted to be alone for a bit curiously enough, given the content of the letter I had just written. So, I went to an arboretum. On the way to the arboretum, I drove through a city, if you could even call it that. The poverty was almost unbearable. People were standing in the street at every red light asking for money, children were playing in the dumpsters, and old men and women sat on the curbs fighting over a small piece of bread. My heart broke as I made my way through this city. Trash lined the streets and there was a smell of stale urine. The whole place was gray with disease. At one red light, a man attacked another and began to beat him right next to the window of my car. I screamed and began to cry. I just wanted to find some nature. There is no way this place has anything quite so beautiful, I thought to myself.

As I looked for a place to turn around without having to go down a back alley, I came across my destination. There was a large fence containing the first green I had seen up to that point. It was as if color had been placed in a world of black and white. The fence seemed to stretch for miles, and I began to work my way around the fence in my car. The arboretum formed a circle and, as I found out later on a map, it sat almost directly in the center of this city. I finally came to the entrance. There was a single large gate standing wide open, and I decided to drive through it. It was like entering an entirely new world. On either side of the road was an immaculate garden, well-groomed and full of life. I was astonished and could barely believe my eyes. There was not a single piece of trash in the garden, and the trees grew so high that the polluted sky seemed far off and almost imaginary now. I parked my car and got out. Would you believe I was the only one in the garden so far as I could tell? The parking lot was empty besides my car, and it stopped right in front of a beautiful house. I walked up to the door and knocked. A tall, old man came to the door and welcomed me inside.

I entered and he proceeded to offer me hot chocolate or coffee. The man's house was so warm and inviting. I trusted him the moment I walked in the door. I took some hot chocolate and sat next to the fireplace. The man went into another room and brought out some maps of the garden he had just printed out. He explained he was the owner and caretaker of the entire arboretum. He told me he had grown up in that city, and he had made his way by hard work and a bit of good luck. He made a fortune on the stock market, and when it came time to retire, he decided to give back to his community. He moved into the center of the community and set up a free arboretum for all of the city's inhabitants to come and experience nature.

I admired that man; he was truly something special. Apparently, much of the arboretum was left from some years ago when the city was first founded, and he set it right again. He invited me to walk around if I liked, and so I did. I wandered that arboretum for hours right up until it closed. Everything there was so beautiful—every plant, every squirrel, and every pond. Once the arboretum closed, the man thanked me for coming and told me to come back anytime. I intend to take you there as soon as you return.

Well, to get home, I had to drive through that horrible city again. The crime, stench, and sadness there still hung like a thick blanket of smog in the air, but I now had a hope that I did not have before. I am sure the metaphorical nature of this arboretum has not eluded your sight, because it did not mine.

This world is dark. Sin pervades every part of human existence, and there is nothing left untouched by the pain that comes with it; I hope to be an arboretum amid this pain. I want to be a speck of light shining for all to see. One small place where hope will seep through the cracks of this broken sidewalk of a world. God has left us here to share His love with everyone and I will leave my gate wide open so any man, woman, or child may come in and have a reprieve from the dark city. Just like with everything else of this world though, my garden will fade. If it were I that was providing the hope, then my inevitable departure would eliminate any positive impact I wish to leave, as I would just take it with me. Rather, the light shining in me and the life living *in me is not my own but comes from Him and His presence in me. Even after I have left this place, His love and hope will remain and will live on in those who love Him. If hope is what you seek, then you need look no further. Humanity's only hope is and always has been in Christ and in Him alone. All the love, joy, and peace in the world is a gift from Him. Any time you see the light of life coming through the cracks of existence, it belongs to Him.*

My arboretum will sit among the lost and I will call them to repentance and hope in Him. I have found my meaning. I have found my life. I have found my joy. I have found Him. Praise God I was not left in the dark city. Praise God that He loves us. We do not deserve it. I do not deserve it.

Anyway, Nathan, come home. I want you to share in my joy and I want you to walk through life with me. I will be waiting for you when you return. Stay safe and come back in one piece.

In Christ,

Emily

Nathan turned to the driver and began to cry. The world began to spin, and Nathan felt himself rising from his seat. The driver rose with him. At once, Nathan remembered everything. Everything the driver had described was not a story at all but was Nathan's life. The ferry hit the dock and the captain came down: standing before Nathan was the man from the side of the road. He was tall, strong, and in his eyes was the heavy burden of love. The captain reached out both of his hands, so Nathan and the driver took them. The captain spoke with words so divine they could not be remembered, but Nathan knew two things: this captain loved him, and he was looking at the face of God. Nathan collapsed to the ground and hugged the captain's feet. He heard the captain crying loudly and knew they were tears of joy. He had caught His pike. His son was home.

Nathan felt the arms of the captain reach down and pick him up off of the ground. He felt himself being carried like a small child off the ferry. All around Nathan the sounds of singing and shouting rang out. Nathan's nose was filled with a pleasing aroma. Nathan was home. He was placed down on something incredibly soft, and Nathan opened his eyes and saw the driver lying there next to him, but now, it was much more like looking into a mirror. The driver reached into his jacket and pulled out one last letter. This one was different, though. It was tattered and worn as if it had been read hundreds of times. The seal was already broken, and the letters had bent corners, so the envelope bulged at its center. Nathan reached out and took the letter from the driver's hand and looked at the front. There was no picture on the cover and Nathan felt this letter was going to be the final thing he ever wanted to read.

Nine

Love's End

Nathan felt a pain in his side and turned over hoping to relieve the pain. He felt the same pain in his back and this time, it was more painful. Nathan, now awake, found himself in the backseat of a Ford. It was his Ford. Nathan turned to see his son standing outside of the car. He was prodding Nathan awake with a cane. "Dad, it's time to go inside. We're here."

Nathan was confused for a second, but then gained composure of himself. He sat up and placed one foot outside of the car and then the other.

"Here—take this, Dad."

Nathan's son handed him his cane. There was such concern behind his son's eyes. Nathan's heart broke to have his son see him like this. Nathan was old and frail. He had a thick beard with deep wrinkles covering his face. Most notably though, Nathan was a man who carried a heavy heart. It was evident in every move he made. He arose from the car and leaned on the cane.

His steps were unsteady and cautious. Nathan paused, lifted his jacket hood, and placed it back onto his head to protect himself from the snow. Bent over, he began to shuffle toward the doors of the chapel. The front of the modern building featured six tall glass doors, each opening into a central room with high reaching ceilings. It would have been pretty under any other circumstance. The chapel's doors were propped open and Nathan walked right in. Nathan was fully aware of his breath and his heartbeat. He tried to maintain his composure, but with each step, this task became more difficult. His heart felt old and his hands and legs trembled. In the lobby of the building sat an easel, tall and well-decorated. Nathan's breath stopped as he noticed what was on it: a picture of Emily. She looked happy, young, and alive. In the background of the picture, Nathan saw himself facing her. Emily was seated on a fallen tree, smiling at the camera, and Nathan was behind her, leaning on a separate tree. There was only love in his eyes as he looked at her. Nathan caught a glimpse of his reflection in the glass covering the image. The same love sat in his eyes now. Below the picture was a plaque that read, "In memory of Emily Stevens." Nathan began to weep. *So, she's really gone,* Nathan thought to himself.

Memories of her death began to flood Nathan's mind and he lost himself as he remembered. He heard a squeaky wheel of a gurney pass by the door of room 435. He was startled by the sound; it caused him to wake up and begin to open his eyes. He opened them slightly and then quickly closed them again, as the light shone brightly through the crack beneath the door and his eyes had not yet adjusted. His back ached, his head throbbed, and his stomach growled. He had been at the hospital for weeks and had grown tired of the food; he had not eaten for a day. He turned to his wife who was laying in the bed beside him and thought, *she is so beautiful.* His eyes remained fixed on her sleeping face. Flowers lined the windowsill and mountains of gifts sat unopened around the room. Decorations hung from the ceiling and get-well cards were hung on the wall across the room. He felt the sounds of the hospital flood his consciousness. The groans of people in pain, the cries of families saying good-bye, the rhythmic beeping of the heart monitor. With every beep, Nathan thanked God that it was not the last. Dread welled up in him as he imagined the last beep and the eerie silence that would follow.

One long tone hummed in Nathan's ears. That moment was frozen in Nathan's mind. Ice filled the room and Nathan's heart stopped. All at once, a flurry of movement erupted as doctors flooded the room and pushed Nathan aside. They began attempting to resuscitate his wife, but the tone just kept ringing. After several minutes the doctors left. Only Nathan and one nurse remained in the room. Nathan gave her an uneasy smile in an attempt to hide his pain. He tried to hold on to his last vestige of control, of his composure, but his grip loosened. The raging torrent of emotions that welled up within him could not be contained. All at once, Nathan's smile turned to a frown and he broke down into tears, falling into the nurse's arms. Nathan had never cried like this. He felt humiliated, weak, and exposed. It was as if his tears had taken over his entire body. He had no control over them; they just kept coming. It felt like his mind was no longer under his control but was hijacked by the most awful pain he had ever experienced. Just then, Nathan began to cry more loudly as the memory faded from the forefront of his mind. Nathan remembered his pain as he stood in the chapel and his son quickly came alongside him and asked, "Are you okay, Dad?"

Nathan turned to look at his son. He saw her in his eyes. Nathan wanted to tell his son he loved him, but Nathan could not stop crying, even for a moment.

"Dad, it's just another sparrow. Isn't that what mom always said?"

Nathan smiled for a brief moment. His son had given him a glimpse of joy and though it may have been only for a moment, Nathan was thankful for the man standing beside him.

"Yes, that's right, son," Nathan said through tears.

With the help of his son, Nathan found his seat inside the auditorium. Nathan sat facing the back of the room. He watched person after person fill the room. *There must be thousands of people here,* Nathan thought to himself. The service started and Nathan remained seated in the front row as people came to greet him and pay their condolences. He felt in a daze, disassociated from what was going on all around him. His children stood to his left and right, greeting people and crying. After some time, everyone found their seats and a man got up and addressed those who had come, but Nathan did not listen. He could not pull his eyes away from the faces of his children who were in such pain. At that moment Nathan cried out, *Father, I need you.* Then he heard someone say,

"Nathan, the husband of Emily, would like to say a few words."

Nathan began to panic; he did not know what to say. What could he say? How could he give hope to a room filled with such pain? Then Nathan, feeling an edge of something pressing against his chest, reached into his jacket pocket. He pulled out an envelope wrapped in a piece of paper. Two of Nathan's sons came over to him, lifted him from his seat, and helped onto the podium.

Nathan unwrapped the envelope, placed it on the lectern, and began to speak. "My son drove me here in my old Ford. Would you believe I've had that Ford since freshman year of college? Anyway, the mechanic says it's on its last leg. Only a few more miles left I suppose, but it got me here." Nathan's voice broke with emotion and so he paused and caught himself. His voice was hoarse, yet it commanded the attention of every person in the room. Even some people walking by the outside of the church stopped to listen.

"That car has been with me for a long time. It was with me when I started college. It was with me when I met my best friend. It was with me when she fell in love with me, and I didn't know it. It was with me when I made the most foolish choice I've ever made: not to love her back immediately. It was with me when I made the best decision I have ever made, to marry her. I guess it wouldn't be there forever, though..."

Nathan's voice trailed off again and he placed his hand over his eyes and pressed his fingers against them. He wanted to speak, but he knew if he did, nothing would come out but faint sounds of shallow breathing.

After a few moments, Nathan spoke a few more words. "But it was there when I received this letter from her."

Nathan held up a small blue envelope, took the letter from it and began to read. He was now able to speak because focusing on reading distracted him from the emotion in what he was saying.

"Dear Nathan,

Alright. Here is my updated list: seven things I look for in a husband. One: must love and love Jesus. Two: takes initiative and is inventive. Three: is uplifting and encouraging. Four: argumentative."

On this one, Nathan stopped and laughed. One shoulder rose, followed by the other, and then they both fell. Nathan found true joy when he read this line.

"I guess this is why she married me."

The audience all laughed with Nathan. He continued.

"Five: doesn't bother over material possessions. Six: pursues curiosity. Seven: seeks to self-improve. After you called me, I called and talked to my friend Max about the whole 'dating your brother' thing."

Nathan stopped to explain. "I may have called her from my trip to the mountains right before I came home, and I also may have told her to date my little brother." The crowd laughed, and Nathan continued to read.

"Well, before I could get into all of that, Max was so interested in hearing my testimony. He said when he was in high school, he considered converting to Christianity because he saw it as an easy way out of being ridiculed for being Muslim. Christianity is definitely not the place to go if you want to avoid ridicule, but besides that, I spent an hour sharing with him stories of all the things Jesus has done for me, and I think it went really well! He says he feels very content at where he is now, but I'll talk to him later today to see what that means. I definitely felt content in high school and the first semester of college. If I was content now, I'd be sitting down, basking in the sun. But I am not. I am sprinting towards and chasing after Jesus. I would not describe myself as content."

Nathan stopped talking and stared at the letter.

"She was sprinting towards Him!" Nathan yelled through his tears as he shook the letter. Nathan missed her so greatly at that moment that his heart broke anew. He felt he might just curl up into a ball and never speak again, but Nathan's oldest son came alongside him, placed his arm around his shoulders, and whispered in his ear,

"Do you want to sit back down, Dad?"

Nathan thought *yes* for a moment, but then he saw his daughter's face. It was purple. He smelled her pain in the air and he could hear every word of pain she was whispering to herself. Then Nathan heard the living words of the driver, "Give them a reason to hope." That was all Nathan had left to do. He needed to show them all that the hope of Emily's life did not merely exist because of her, but because of her hope in Christ. Nathan needed to tell them this, but he also needed to hear it himself. Nathan turned to his son and said in a shaky and uneasy voice,

"No, thank you, I will finish."

Then Nathan turned toward the microphone and continued reading.

"Anyway, no, I can't date your brother because I keep lying to myself and saying I don't actually have feelings for you when I know full well I do. So, you may have a handful of reasons why I should date your brother, but I have a multitude of reasons why you should date me, and that's that. I am not about to turn this into some kind of love letter, but I am going to send this one off in the mail while I still have the courage and before I convince myself not to. In Christ, Emily."

Nathan placed the letter down on the lectern in front of him and took a deep breath. He felt his whole life would find its meaning at this moment. The moment where he reminded the world that Emily's life was not her own but was God's.

"Emily loved three things. She loved Jesus, her children, and her husband. Not one of those things does she leave unfulfilled because she loved them through Christ, and Christ's hope will always live on as long as hope is needed because Christ lives."

Nathan stepped down from the podium and slowly made his way back to where he was seated. The rest of the day was a blur for Nathan; he must have spoken to a thousand people and heard thousands more speak of Emily's great impact. As the day drew to a close, Nathan knew his life must now go on without Emily. One truth remained firmly planted in Nathan's mind—Christ loved him, and His love was more powerful than any number of sparrows.

THE END